MILE 2

31 EXTRA MILE SECRETS

FOR AN EXTRAORDINARY LIFE

STEVE WARNER

Praise for *Mile 2*

"Most of us want success without the prerequisite sacrifice. But that isn't the way it works. After all, the difference between ordinary and extraordinary is extra. And that is certainly true of the extra mile mindset that Steve Warner advocates. This countercultural challenge can lead to an extraordinary life."

~ **Mark Batterson**, New York Times best-selling author of The Circle Maker, The Grave Robber, A Trip around the Sun, and If.

"Steve Warner does an amazing job of bringing this important truth to the forefront again by resurrecting it for a generation that has too often jettisoned Mile 2 behavior as a lifestyle. The author rightly says that those who go the extra mile tend to thrive in life. Steve Warner illustrates this timely truth by using colorful biblical and secular examples, especially from the life of Jesus. The riveting stories effectively highlight and illustrate the 31 secrets. His book is a must read!"

~ **Dr. Bill Jeynes**, Professor of Education at California State University, Long Beach, author of 12 books, numerous articles and academic publications.

"Most of us have difficulty putting the concept of extra mile living into daily practice. Thankfully, Dr. Warner's insightful book discloses one relevant and practical 'Mile 2 secret' for each day of the month. His recommendations for going the extra mile can now be applied on a daily basis — for the benefit of others and ourselves."

~ **Dr. Wayne Westcott**, author of 25 fitness books, including Strength Training Past 50, Building Strength and Stamina.

MILE 2

31 Extra Mile Secrets for an Extraordinary Life

1st Edition

Mile 2 Publications

East Bridgewater, MA

rswarner1@comcast.net

ISBN: 978-0-9969971-0-2 (paperback)

ISBN: 978-0-9969971-1-9 (eBook)

Scripture quotations, unless otherwise indicated, are taken from The Holy Bible, *New International Version®*, NIV® Copyright ©1973, 1978, 1984, 2011 by Biblica, Inc.® All rights reserved worldwide.

Dedication

Dedicated to my wife, Vickie, who personifies the Extra Mile secrets contained in this book better than anyone I know.

MILE 2

Contents

Preface

Before We Start Hiking Mile 2

No one begins life as an Extra Miler.

In fact, right after we emerge from the womb we can't cover our first steps without assistance, much less even a fraction of the first mile.

We can't walk and must be carried everywhere. We cry and sleep a lot, demand constant attention, and do nothing to help others. "Please" and "thank you" aren't in our vocabulary because we don't talk. The world revolves around us and our needs because we haven't learned civility. It never occurs to us that waking our parents up in the middle of the night is a tad inconvenient. Our manners leave a lot to be desired.

In fact, life is all about us.

At some point we begin to mature. We learn to talk, walk, and think. We reciprocate. (If you scratch my back I'll scratch yours. If you treat me nicely I'll be nice to you, too.) However, we are still on the one-mile road. Our aim isn't to serve but to be served.

In so many ways we are still infants in our worldview. The difference is that we've learned to cloak our self-centeredness.

We don't throw tantrums or stomp our feet any longer. But neither do we seek opportunities to go over and beyond.

However, some people make an amazing discovery somewhere along the line. They realize that in the years since they were kicking the slats out of the cradle their philosophy of life has changed. It isn't any longer about them, but about others. The goal is no longer to walk one uneventful mile, but to go the Extra Mile.

We call this proverbial mile, this second mile – Mile 2.

In the following pages we'll discover 31 secrets eventually known by all people determined to hike the Extra Mile. Living these secrets leads to an extraordinary life.

You can read one chapter a day for a long month or go at your own pace. Either way, welcome to the pilgrimage.

Let's meet at trail's end.

Chapter 1: Extra-Milers Have a Contagious Attitude

"Give and it will be given to you."
~ Jesus as quoted in Luke 6:38

Secret #1

At first the action behind a fast-food counter may appear to be little more than organized chaos. But if you are watching carefully, you'll soon witness a remarkable phenomenon. Several employees will be taking orders; some barking orders; some filling orders. And then there will almost certainly be another group, studiously avoiding orders.

However, the one to take note of is the girl whose badge tells us her name is "Katie". She is not the manager, but she is the one doing more than her share, smiling with her eyes at each customer as she says, "How else can I serve you?" And she is serving not only the customer on the other side of the counter but her co-workers as well, doing whatever it takes to make things run smoothly, providing help wherever it is needed.

The members of the work crew almost imperceptibly align themselves into one of these groups. The distinction may not be obvious at first but what you will ultimately witness is a division of the employees into the ranks of One-Milers or Extra-Milers.

They are not dressed in different uniforms. Their uniqueness won't be written on their name badges, nor will age, sex, or nationality be the defining issues. You will see it in their body language and work ethic.

One-Milers are most noteworthy for merely going through the minimal motions. This group is invariably gifted at imitating dynamism. Though their bodies may be at work, their minds and souls will be elsewhere – at the beach, on a date, sleeping – anywhere but in the moment. They move slowly, gaze at the clock longingly, and mimic work only when absolutely necessary. If someone asks for anything extra, politely or otherwise, the request will almost certainly be met with a shrug and a sigh, body language reflecting objection to additional effort. Neither a smile nor eye contact will come.

Granted, there may not be equal fulfillment for everybody in work of any sort. There are boring jobs. If we're honest, all of us occasionally engage in daydreaming while we work, worship, or play – however important and exciting the assigned or chosen task. But those who are One-Milers, people who do the minimum and not one iota more, have developed work evasion into an art form.

In most cases, a decade from now the One-Milers will still be exhibiting little initiative, and will most likely have little to show for ten years in the work force. One-Milers rarely succeed, not by reason of societal determinism, but because of lack of personal determination.

And then there are the Extra-Milers. They are the diligent, inspired pilgrims; in many cases they are less gifted than their single-mile counterparts. So, what's the difference? Characteristics like initiative, attitude, thoughtfulness and servanthood – that's the difference.

Extra-Milers distinguish themselves. They are turbo-charged. Though they may hold an entry-level employment position at a fast food place, any member of the Extra Mile group will likely be promoted quickly from the ranks to management. It won't be long before they may own the place.

Customers don't have to ask Extra-Milers for anything; it is proactively offered as part of the Extra Mile mindset as their needs are anticipated with a smile, eye contact, and a heartfelt thank you. The customers will return for the attention and kind treatment doled out by the Extra-Milers in any business.

Mile 1 members do the least, resist the most, and think the world has conspired to make them unhappy. Mile 2 people go above and beyond and know the secret to creating an extraordinary life is in the way they bus a table or cook a hamburger, whether it's in Poughkeepsie, Providence, or Provo. You will find both types of people on sales floors, in office buildings, in college classrooms, just about anywhere and everywhere. The net corporate effect of the two groups, for good or ill, is easily tracked in the financial pages of any newspaper. Indeed, almost every section of a paper or magazine – whether sports, entertainment, or general news – essentially reports which of the two groups is ultimately successful.

One-Milers and Extra-Milers spell failure or fruitfulness to families, businesses, churches, and communities in every time zone around the globe. They prove Mark Twain's adage that "the difference between lightning and the lightning bug is in a single word." So, pick your own three-letter word: Will it be one or two miles? Before you make your choice though, think about what is at stake. It's important to face the facts: Most people won't travel the sweaty Extra Mile just because it is a good idea or even because the credo is in the Bible, part of Jesus' famous Sermon on the Mount.

The reality is that almost no one is so altruistic, so selfless. "What are the benefits?" we inevitably want to know. The answer can be summarized succinctly in one word: Success.

Success comes in many shapes and colors. It is not ultimately measured in more dollars or promotions or trophies, though it can be. There are the unmeasurables to consider, such as a sense of accomplishment, the exhilaration of taking a proactive role in one's own destiny, or the warm glow of divine approval that comes when God has been honored by our going further and doing more than was expected.

Remember the scene in the movie Chariots of Fire when Eric Liddle is trying to explain to his religiously inclined sister why running is so important to him? She can't fathom how being a world-class runner is more important than going to China as a missionary. Finally, with restrained exasperation he says to her: "It's because when I run I feel God's pleasure." To her credit, she finally gets the point. For many Extra-Milers the smile of God is enough reward, a sufficient measure of success. It is seldom so for One-Milers.

For Jesus to hear his Father say "I'm pleased with you," was enough, no doubt about it. He didn't need awards or recognition. Maybe it is the same for you too.

However, along with a sense that heaven is beaming down upon us we can also receive more immediate and tangible rewards. This need not be an either/or proposition. A person walking the Extra Mile can simultaneously glorify God and achieve a high degree of temporal satisfaction. The latter may take the form of a pat on the back, a tenured position, money in the bank, a trip to Maui, or rocking a grandchild to sleep.

The story of David and Goliath illustrates that an Extra-Miler can both please God and achieve personal benefits. It's true that David took on the giant because the big guy had mocked his God. But David had also heard that the one who defeated the massive Philistine would be amply rewarded in other ways as well. While David had noble motives before he picked up his slingshot, it didn't hurt that the "wanted poster" for Goliath also included some significant fringe benefits. Let's consider the biblical account...

"Have you seen the giant?" many of the soldiers were asking. "He comes out each day to challenge Israel. And have you heard about the huge reward the king has offered to anyone who kills him? The king will give him one of his daughters for a wife, and his whole family will be exempt from paying taxes!"

David asked those who were standing nearby to verify the report of reward. "What did you just say the man will get for killing this Philistine and putting an end to his abuse of Israel?" David received the same reply as before: "What you have heard is true. There is a huge reward for the one who slays the giant." Their confirmation boosted David's courage. He asked those around him: "Who is this pagan Philistine anyway, that he is allowed to defy the armies of the living God?" The rest is history.

So, while many Extra-Milers go over and beyond for eternal reasons, and while it is true that the joy of Extra Mile living should be enough incentive, there are big perks here and now for doing the right thing." The Extra Mile creates the environment for success, adventure, and promotion. The tedious first mile almost always traps those so disposed in the doldrums of the ordinary, where every day is gray and unremarkable.

Let's take this pop quiz: Think of five people you know whom you would rate as successful. Write their names on a piece of paper. Now, what sets them apart in your mind? Why do you think that they made the cut to be on your list? Why do you admire them more than the others you thought of, but didn't write down?

I daresay that all five of them typically go over and beyond the call of duty somehow. They are all Extra-Milers and each one, in his or her own way, is eminently successful. And successful people, whether rich or poor, famous or unknown, share the distinction of fleshing out the mandate of Jesus: "If someone forces you to go one mile, go with him two miles."

I have led and pastored churches for much of my life. Within the ranks of those who fill the pews are many One-Milers and not a few Extra-Milers. Here's the way it often works. The former spell service, "serve-us". They sign up for church membership so they can have one of the ministers on retainer. The prevailing attitude among this segment of the congregation is "I'll let you know if and when you're needed, Rev." They'll periodically feel guilty (usually following a sermon about commitment), and "volunteer" to clean up after a fellowship dinner or visit a shut-in sporadically. But most of the time they do little more than cover the backs of the barren pews, and then only when it is convenient to their schedules.

By contrast, the Extra Mile parishioners have a wholly (and holy) different theology. They come in the door, scanning those assembled like Secret Service agents, looking for people they can help, searching for a need to meet and a hurt to soothe. It's not that this cadre is the wealthiest or the healthiest. (Indeed, in many cases it's the opposite.) They have simply adopted an Extra Mile lifestyle, one that embodies this often-ignored tenet of faith, which reaches far beyond the limits of Christianity or mere do-goodism. Take Charlotte, for example. One Sunday she met a visiting couple from Nigeria in the lobby of the church I was pastoring at the time. They expressed appreciation for her friendliness, and then remarked to her that they had thoroughly enjoyed the corporate singing time. Wistfully, they mentioned how much they'd like to have one of our nice hymnals. Where could they buy one?

Well, the hymnals weren't for sale. But Charlotte took things into her own hands. She asked one of the staff pastors, who was nearby, if she could give away a hymnal. She offered to defray the cost herself. Emboldened by an affirmative answer, she presented the gift to our foreign guests.

When she told me about the experience, she could hardly contain her joy. Her offer to repay the church coffers for the book was kind, but unnecessary. Charlotte had shown herself to be a true Extra-Miler. She had come upon a problem and solved it. She had seen an opportunity and responded to it positively and proactively.

However, the story didn't end there. The following morning, the African couple, on their way to the airport to jet back to their homeland, stopped by my office to express appreciation. They gushed about Charlotte's generosity, and noted that such thoughtfulness must certainly be part of the DNA of the entire church. Would I write something in the flyleaf of the hymnal, they asked, so they could remember their positive visit once back in Lagos? I did so most happily, realizing that there will be more to their story, one that started casually with a caring parishioner going the Extra Mile.

Such courtesies occur daily across America on numerous levels. In business they make the difference between a one-time purchase and a longtime customer. For the salesperson it can mean the difference between a nice commission and base pay. In marriage it can spell the difference between divorce and a golden wedding anniversary. In sports it can be the difference between the Hall of Fame and a mere asterisk in the record books.

Some companies and employees have so excelled at the Extra Mile ideal that their names are synonymous with customer satisfaction. I imagine that even now the names of such stores, airlines, and corporations came to mind. Furthermore, you likely wouldn't have picked up this book if you weren't already well on your way from Milepost One to Milepost Two (or at least desiring to start the journey on the Extra Mile).

People on the Extra Mile instinctively, almost irresistibly, long to improve and excel. You, the reader of this book, are my kind of person and more importantly, the kind of person who makes both God and the world sit up and take notice.

So this book is not only for you; it is about you. It is both the story of others and your story, too. It is history in the making, both biography and autobiography. And it contains an element of the prophetic, since it foretells what we can do if we will only try just a bit harder.

A person on the Extra Mile is an individual with a special attitude, not necessarily a specific aptitude. Extra-Milers don't memorize precepts and recite mantras. There are no dues for membership in our loosely knit organization. There is no formal application to fill out. You will be glad to know that there aren't a string of dos and don'ts to heed or shun. The only absolute requirement is the cultivation of the habit to keep walking when you've hit the normal human limit that awaits all of us at the single-mile marker.

What follows in the next 30 chapters is an explanation of how the Extra Mile attitude can permeate everything we do every day, in every situation. Whatever our goal, this book is for everyone, as anyone can have that attitude. I believe that we should be continually challenged to do better, and we can encourage those we serve to do the same. So, as we start this journey, I'm convinced that you and I are of kindred hearts. Since we're going in the same direction, for the same distance, can we make the trip together?

Our mutual goal is Mile 2. Let's keep walking.

Chapter 2: Extra-Milers Are One-Milers Who Decide to Go Two

"If someone forces you to go one mile, go with him
two miles."
~ Jesus in the Sermon on the Mount

Secret # 2

Most of us are not big on dos and don'ts. There is a part of all of us that resists asking for or taking directions, especially if the directions come in the form of commands. We would just as soon find our own way, our own "truth", sometimes at the risk of meandering around in circles or even getting lost.

For example, many view the Ten Commandments as antiquated intrusions into our modern-day lifestyle. The litany of "thou shalt nots" raises the hackles of those who demand "please consider" or "think about this" as preface to any instruction. However, relatively few take offense at the wisdom of the Sermon on the Mount, even though the precepts found therein are arguably far more than a mere compilation of practical suggestions.

Two thousand years ago on a balmy afternoon the most quoted man in history made a startling declaration. It is still nestled in a single line within the larger context of that famous sermon. It's easy to miss: "If a soldier tries to make you take his knapsack for one mile, volunteer to carry it for – two miles!"

Jesus wasn't addressing a sales convention or a political rally. Nor was his aim to motivate a mediocre football team to get off the bench and score some touchdowns. Jesus' powerful and pithy talk went well beyond merely trying to instill a can-do attitude in his sizeable audience.

When he spoke these words Jesus' focus was mainly spiritual. Midway through this revolutionary speech his words reached a heightened level of intensity. Just when his listeners were ready to put aside their prejudices against yet another to-do list, the attentive Jewish crowd thought they heard him say the unthinkable: "If someone forces you to go one mile, go with him two miles." What? Excuse me? Say again?

Jesus may have repeated the line again, more slowly this time, for added emphasis: "You heard me right. If someone forces you to go one mile, then go two miles!"

At first members of the audience may have concluded that they had heard Jesus incorrectly and muttered: "Teacher, teacher, certainly you jest. You can't mean it. Say it isn't so, rabbi." Certainly this increasingly popular instructor had not suggested going a willing Extra Mile with a despised Roman centurion! It was unthinkable that a Jew, especially a well-liked teacher, would speak such heresy. The Romans were hated by every true Jew. They certainly weren't to be obeyed. They were to be despised.

So each person must have filled in the final words at the end of Jesus' sentence with any number of alternate endings to the one-mile-versus-two-mile dictum Jesus had just uttered.

If we had been among the crowd listening on the hill that day, we may have heard and seen the following scenarios...

A zealot murmuring that Jesus must have meant to say: "If someone forces you to go one mile ... spit on him! Don't give in to the foreign oppressors. Resist the Roman dogs. Let all of them carry their own knapsacks."

A teenage boy likely concluding that Jesus meant to say: "If someone forces you to go one mile ... glare at him. If you must carry the pack do it badly. Scuff it along the ground. Old Sarge will be glad when the required single mile is up. He'll never ask you to help him again – and his luggage will be ruined, too."

The rabbi probably hearing him say: "If someone forces you to go one mile quote some messianic prophesies to him out of the Old Testament. Let him know a powerful leader will one day come to liberate us, the Chosen People. Beat him over the head with the Torah!"

But what Jesus had said he clearly meant to say. He wasn't hyperbolizing. He refused to edit his words to suit the audience spread out before him on the hillside that afternoon.

He said: "If someone forces you to go one mile with him, go two miles."

If Jesus had political aspirations, that additional little three-word tag, the one containing the Extra Mile mandate, relegated him to the back of the line as a potential vote getter. His declaration was the dynamic equivalent of a modern candidate saying, "If elected I'm going to raise taxes the very first thing." Members of that Jewish crowd, who had traversed significant distances to hear the popular teacher, were probably at first incredulous, then indignant.

So what was the big deal about the Extra Mile law?

At that time Palestine was under Roman rule. To show a feisty Jewish zealot who was really in charge, Roman soldiers would frequently invoke a law intended to demean the citizens of that proud, downtrodden little country. The law gave Roman soldiers the right to compel civilians to carry their heavy packs for a "milion", the rough equivalent of our modern mile. The rub was in the odious word "compel".

The arrangement was disruptive to a worker's day. It was insensitive to the aged and the infirm. But the most obvious intent was to make the conquered bear the burdens of their sneering conquerors. It was meant to further humiliate an already-vanquished country, to add insult to injury.

"If someone forces you…" The verb Jesus used, meaning to compel, was particularly offensive. It was a borrowed word from the Persian language. To the Medo-Persians it had meant "to conscript for service against one's will." The term originated with the ancient Persian postal service.

Persian governmental workers were expected to deliver the mail on time. So important was punctual mail delivery to the Persians that mailmen could be hanged for failing to do so. Hence, the early mail carriers were given authority to press into service a person, his or her horse, or anything else deemed necessary to expedite the hasty delivery of the mail.

However, there were obvious potential abuses inherent in such a system. The temptation to use the law for selfish reasons was great. The postman's badge began to be flashed for personal rather than proper reasons. The line between governmental and personal use of this perk became blurred.

Then Rome dipped back in history and revived this old Persian law. Roman soldiers were given the right to compel the vanquished to carry their packs. Eventually what was once the often misused prerogative of the Persian postman, who sometimes forced an unwitting person along his route to cater to his whims, had become a finely honed science within the ranks of the Roman military force encamped in Judea and Galilee.

Fortunately the law had its limits. The writ of Rome allowed for a forced march of one mile – and only one mile. At the end of a single Roman milion (about 5000 feet) the unwilling bearer of the knapsack could legally call it quits. You were entitled to say (albeit in dolce voce): "Get some other human mule to tote your load, corporal. I'm finished for the day. I know my rights, although they may be few and far between."

With the requirement of the law met, the angry teen could commiserate with his youthful friends. The wealthy businessman, his nice linen robe irreparably soiled from the unwanted and unexpected burden of a bulging backpack, might brush himself off and return to his personal business, his schedule now rendered useless by the unwelcome intrusion.

The first mile was hard enough. So who would ever voluntarily invite the imposition of an Extra Mile? Some of the people on the hillside that day were no doubt thinking, "How dare this upstart prophet from backwater Nazareth preach such a non-kosher message? Whose side is he on anyway? Is he a Roman agent – or just an insensitive rube? Away with him and his unwelcome ideas!"

Two millennia have provided sufficient time for the dissenting voices to be silenced. That first indignant throng intermingled with the ashes and the dirt long ago. The Romans have become dust on the floor of history. No one has been forced to carry a legionnaire's pack for over seventeen centuries. That ancient rule is now powerless and officially moot. However, the Extra Mile mandate, at least in principle, is definitely not outdated.

There are still naysayers who argue that the minimum is enough. "One mile will do," they say. Yet, the jury of time and experience has returned another verdict. Jesus was right. He still is. Those who are travelers on the Extra Mile end up the winners in every way. The effects of the Extra Mile maxim are transcultural and transcendent. Two miles are perennially better than one. The Extra Mile is where careers are made, long-standing records are broken, and advancement is secured.

Of course, the starting point these days is not at a literal milepost by a roadside, but an invisible marker within the heart. The Extra Mile is an attitude; a philosophy of life; a part of one's practical theology fleshed out, not in cathedrals or churches, but where Main Street meets Broadway.

Make no mistake here. Mile 2 is not about manipulation, mere customer service, or cheap flattery. Nor is it a means to a selfish personal end. If the ultimate good of the person we are serving is not in focus, then the point of the additional mile is lost and with it the blessing that its application can bring.

Harry Emerson Fosdick shares about the occasion when his mother sent him to pick berries. Her instructions were non-negotiable: Pick at least a quart of raspberries before you come home. As a young man there were many things higher on Harry's priority list than filling a quart bucket with tiny berries. So he confesses that his attitude was less than joyful as he trudged into the field, to comply with what he felt was an unreasonable demand. His only goal was to get the task accomplished as quickly as possible, thereby to be released to play with his friends.

Then he was struck by a strange and unfamiliar inspiration. What if he voluntarily picked two quarts instead of just one? Wouldn't the family, especially his mother, be surprised?

Years later he reflected: "I had so interesting a time picking two quarts of raspberries, to the utter amazement of the household, that, although it happened a half-century ago, I have never forgotten [the lesson that] what the circumstances and compulsions of life do to us depends upon what they find in us."

Fosdick had discovered the idea of Extra Mile living. He had learned the value of trekking freely and willingly along XX, the Extra Mile road. People on this less traveled road are simply one-milers who one day decided they would go two – and they haven't stopped or looked back since. One day you're reluctantly picking one quart of berries; the next day you are joyfully filling two buckets. One day you're doing the minimum; the next day you refuse to settle for anything less than the maximum.

What has occurred? You have made the choice to go the Extra Mile willingly, joyfully, fueled not by writ but by will. You have decided to be proactive, rather than reactive. From now on a Roman soldier may call you to carry his pack, but you'll be the one who determines both your attitude and the distance of the journey. The idea of abdicating your newfound good cheer in exchange for a victim mentality is suddenly and forever anathema. You will take charge by going the Extra Mile, the unrequired additional milion that leaves Roman soldiers of all eras speechless, powerless, and more than a little confused.

But doubling the obligatory first mile requires intentionality. This formula for mile multiplication seldom occurs of its own accord. There is no mistaking the Extra Mile for the first one. They are as different as day and night. The first mile is a taskmaster fueled by extrinsic motivation. But the Extra Mile is hiked to the rhythm of intrinsic motivation. There is a significant difference between the two. The former is about being forced to behave in a certain way; the latter is about desiring to act in a specific manner.

Drudgery hallmarks the first mile; desire fuels the Extra Mile.

A young Native American lad wanted to become a respected mature member of his tribe. The problem was his lifelong fear of the dark. So, when he approached the tribal council and asked to be given the full privileges of an adult male, he was told he would need to overcome his nighttime phobia first. Later that evening he was given an empty wooden water pail and was instructed to go to the creek and bring it back to the elders brimming full.

He set off running toward the creek in morbid fear, tripping over branches, bruising and scratching himself before he got to the water's edge. Breathlessly he drew the water from the stream and sprinted back to camp with the pail gripped in his trembling hand.

However, when he got back to the camp it was discovered that almost all of the water had spilled out of the pail because of his haste. The older men found this unacceptable. The lad had not heeded their instructions. This was evidence to those in the tribal circle that the young man's fear had not yet been fully conquered.

So he was sent back to the creek again. This time he was so tired from the rigors of his recent one-mile sprint that he walked the path slowly, less out of bravery and more by reason of his exhaustion. As he jogged the path the second time his fears began to subside. He could see the beauty of the forest through the filtered rays of moonlight. The hooting owl sounded less haunting. The shadows no longer took on the forms of imaginary specters. He was at peace. Following the second trip, the tribal council promoted the young man to the rank of full adulthood with all of the attendant rights and honors of such status.

Traveling the Extra Mile may be about doing more or doing less, according to the requirements of the moment. It may mean ceasing to chitchat with a coworker in favor of serving a waiting customer with added efficiency or, on the other hand, it may require slowing down and actually listening to what your daughter is trying to tell you.

Extra-Milers are quite simply one-milers who consciously decide to go two miles instead. The Extra Mile may be a sprint or a stroll, but the real point is that two miles effectively doubles what you would ordinarily have done. As we travel the Extra Mile the honors and promotions come along with the bigger tips, the longer marriages, and the better friendships.

So, let's move further down this Extra Mile and along the way, let's chat about additional changes we may want to consider if we are to become fully vested members of the Extra Mile Club.

Chapter 3: Extra-Milers Have a Change of Attitude along the Way

"As they were going out, they met a man from
Cyrene, named Simon, and they forced him to carry
the cross."
~ St Matthew describing Jesus on the road to his
crucifixion

Secret # 3

On my bookshelf sits a sleek model of the Bell X-1, nicknamed Glamorous Glennis. The real full-scale aircraft is exhibited at The National Air and Space Museum. There's an Extra Mile story behind how it came to be displayed both in my office and in Washington, DC.

Mach 1 – the speed of sound – is 660 miles per hour at 20,000 feet. In the mid-1940s no aircraft had yet flown that fast. In fact, aeronautical engineers called Mach 1 the "sound barrier" because they believed that at such a speed, airloads could cause a plane to break up. But, of course, no one would know for sure until a plane actually flew that fast.

In 1947, the Army Air Corps chose Chuck Yeager as the test pilot for the X-1, the aircraft it hoped would be the one to break Mach 1. Indeed, the rocket engine of the X-1 had the power to push the aircraft close to Mach 2 – if the plane could hold together, and if the control elevators and flaps continued to function properly.

The engineers planned a series of test flights so Yeager could inch gradually toward Mach 1, adding an additional 20 mph with each flight. For a while it didn't look good. The closer Yeager flew to Mach 1, the more problems the X-1 experienced.

At Mach .86 "...it felt like I was driving on bad shock absorbers over uneven paving stones..." Yeager writes in his autobiography. "The right wing suddenly got heavy and began to drop, and when I tried to correct it my controls were sluggish. I increased my speed to Mach .88 to see what would happen. I saw my aileron vibrating with shock waves, and only with effort could I hold my wing level."

During Yeager's seventh flight, as he edged up to Mach .94, he pulled on his control wheel to lift the nose of the X-1. Nothing happened. The controls felt broken. Yeager jettisoned his fuel and landed, fearing he had taken his last flight in the X-1.

Engineers analyzed the flight data and learned that at Mach .94 a shock wave hit one of the control elevators, negating Yeager's control of the aircraft. But they soon discovered how to overcome the problem, and Yeager resumed his relentless advance toward the elusive sound barrier.

The ninth flight was slated for October 14, 1947. The plan was for Yeager to edge up to Mach .97. Yeager had fallen off a horse and broken some ribs, so he was in no mood to fly. Nevertheless he climbed into the B-29 that would carry the X-1 in its bomb bay up to 20,000 feet. When the time came, Yeager gingerly descended down a ladder into the X-1. Once the X-1 dropped away from the B-29 he started the X-1's engines and took off on his own.

At Mach .88 the X-1 began to be buffeted again. Yeager adjusted his stabilizer, things smoothed out, and he continued to accelerate.

"I noticed that the faster I got, the smoother the ride," says Yeager. "Suddenly the Mach needle began to fluctuate. It went up to .965 Mach and then tipped right off the scale. I thought I was seeing things! We were flying supersonic! And it was as smooth as a baby's bottom: Grandma could be sitting up there sipping lemonade. I kept the speed off the scale for about 20 seconds, and then raised the nose to slow down. I was thunderstruck. After all the anxiety, breaking the sound barrier turned out to be a perfectly paved speedway."

Back in the tracking van engineers reported hearing what sounded like a distant rumble of thunder. It was the sound of history being made, the first sonic boom ever produced on earth by a human invention.

The loud noise was more than a scientific phenomenon, however. It was the sound of disintegrating paradigms. Humans could go beyond the sound barrier after all. Mach 2 was achievable. Today scores of pilots break that fabled barrier every single day.

Of course, this story is both history and metaphor. Concerning the latter, the moment any of us push up against the Extra Mile, our personal Mach 2, we break the attitude barrier, and there is a responsive sonic boom of joy. The attitude barrier tries very hard to keep us at the first order of living. But break the attitude barrier, and we can suddenly travel at Mach 2 and beyond with little or no turbulence.

Before we break the attitude barrier we tend to respond in kind: Eye for eye, anemic effort for anemic effort, measure for measure. The lower others sink, the lower we sink, too. We are slaves to the worst and the least. We vie with other single milers to do the minimum, to shrink back from taking risks and trying harder.

Then something happens in us and to us. Suddenly a run-in with a modern day "Roman soldier" becomes a positive encounter; an opportunity for good to triumph over evil, a chance for nobler values to be born. We rise well above the perceived injustice of the situation and the glaring faults of our companions. No matter what others do to us now, we are champions because we have taken upon ourselves far more than a bullying soldier's backpack. We have deliberately shouldered a new attitude, birthed not by negative reaction to a foe, nor even as a concession to the inevitable, but as a willing embrace of an opportunity that can spell success when seen from our new vantage point.

Imagine one of the men – we'll call him Simon – leaving the hill by the Sea of Galilee that day, where he has just heard the most amazing and perplexing sermon of his life, preached by a young rabbi named Jesus. The year is 30 AD. His scroll is overflowing with notes. If he tries to live out even one of the ideas he has just heard it will demand that he concede to radical inner transformation. He thinks about the memorable line about going an Extra Mile, even when required by law to trudge only one mile.

He decides to experiment with this suggestion the next time he is ordered to tote a bag for the required mile. Simon tells himself that today, just this once, he will go two miles instead of the single one ordered by Roman law. In so doing he will prove the upstart teacher's theories to be impractical drivel. If he can disprove this single point in the sermon, he reasons, the rest can be safely discarded as well. Then he won't be so troubled about the other challenging statements that were made that afternoon.

Though still doubting the truth of what he has heard, Simon becomes increasingly anxious to test the Extra Mile ideal as soon as possible. So, on the way back to his home, he goes out of his way to attract the attention of a Roman infantryman who is resting by the roadside atop his army-issue haversack. He hasn't long to wait, for with the all-too familiar imperial wave of a calloused hand, the soldier wordlessly points Simon toward his heavy, well-traveled leather bag. "Carry it – for a mile," he says slowly, sneering.

Simon can't make out the rank of the man whose pack he now carries. The badge of merit sewn to his cape bears the familiar eagle with the Roman C below the claws. No matter, he's the enemy, whatever his rank or lack of it. They're all the same, these Latin-speaking pig-eating Romans, thinks Simon.

The unwritten rule during these mile-long forced marches was that they were to be performed in silence. There was no communication of any kind allowed, not even eye contact. Latin and Aramaic were as incompatible as the Romans and Jews who spoke the languages. Why even try a conversation with a barbaric Roman legionnaire?

So they trudge along blanketed in heavy silence, the soldier and the zealot. Simon spends the first half-mile wondering what possessed him to actually invite the placement of this chafing load on his shoulders. He can feel the weapons move within the knapsack. He can hear the clinking of their metal. He can only imagine how many of his countrymen they have injured or even killed. Every few steps Simon is tempted to throw the sack down, reach into its folds, draw out a knife or short sword from within its dank interior, and dispatch the sneering Roman to Hades with his own armament.

In the midst of his reverie, Simon suddenly hears himself say: "Captain" (it doesn't hurt to "promote" the soldier you are serving) "do you have family back in Rome?"

Never before has Simon proactively addressed a Roman civilly. To make matters worse, what he blurts out was in broken Latin of such laughable quality that Simon braces himself for instant ridicule from the soldier. However, to his amazement, the soldier doesn't laugh. He doesn't sneer. He looks stunned. The look is akin to the one Simon imagined moments before, when he had been daydreaming about running the fellow through with his own sword. In that moment Simon had mentally seen the soldier fall, his hand on the hilt of the buried dagger. Simon had imagined the Roman's face registering perplexity along with pain, silently mouthing the words: "How have you become the master and I the servant?" But even though no weapon has been employed Simon now sees that look on the soldier's face as he attempts to initiate a conversation with him.

When he finally finds his voice the Roman centurion hoarsely responds that he does indeed have family in Rome. He volunteers that his wife is often sick and their youngest son has fainting fits. He has not been home in three years. But if he is granted a New Year's wish, he and all one hundred of his men will soon find themselves back beside the Tiber River, far from this suffocating dung-and-dust bowl called Judea.

It has never occurred to Simon that some Romans might actually not want to be in Palestine. So he tentatively asks yet another question in broken Latin. The centurion answers him in even worse Aramaic. This imaginary dialogue between enemies, unrecorded by history, continues until the soldier brusquely says, "Mile's up."

It is Simon's turn to be perplexed. "What mile?"

Centurion: "The one that the law of compulsion requires."

Simon: "What if I want to go another mile with you, Centurion, sir?"

Centurion: "I've never, ever had anyone ask such a question, zealot. I said that the mile is up. You are free to leave. You know the law. Now, go!"

Simon: "Would you mind terribly if I went with you another milion?"

Centurion: "In all my years of marching for Rome I've never had such a strange request. Are you mocking me, Jew?"

Simon: "No. No, sir. I would just like to finish our conversation. Let me carry your bag while we finish chatting, if you don't mind. Is that alright with you?"

As the Centurion pauses to rub his hand over his weathered sunburned face he says: "Ah, well, if you insist. But I don't know what has come over you since I compelled you to carry my bags a mile back. What's the catch? What are you up to?"

What has happened in Simon is an overwhelming change of attitude along the way. It happens to all those who walk the Extra Mile, usually sometime during the first uneventful mile. Odometer watching suddenly stops. The serendipitous journey begins. The incremental markers beside the road, the ones that the hiker once relied upon to measure when the indignity of carrying the pack would mercifully end, somehow become inconsequential.

The centurion may not immediately become a friend, but he's no longer an ogre. Likewise, the teacher, the boss, the pastor, the employee, the spouse, the customer are all transformed as if by some formula of spiritual alchemy. Two miles are discovered to always be superior to one, if the pack-carrier's attitude becomes transformed within the framework of the first onerous mile.

Simon learned his lesson. Having incorporated it into his daily life, he returned to his native Cyrene on business. When he next returned to Judea I imagine that he may have been given a very public forum to exhibit the validity of Jesus' teaching about the Extra Mile, which he had first heard and then actually practiced, on that balmy Galilean afternoon.

For as I see the story unfold, the Simon of our story may have been one and the same as Simon of Cyrene, who is known to history as the man who was compelled to carry the cross for Jesus. If so, was it a mere coincidence that Simon returned to Jerusalem on the exact day when Jesus needed help carrying his heavy cross further than most would have willingly journeyed?

Did the centurion pick Simon out of the crowd because he recognized him as someone he knew who had developed the habit of traveling the Extra Mile, even for a dying stranger? And does the biblical narrative use the verb "compel" to describe Simon's service as random or deliberate? It is, after all, the same hated verb Jesus used three years before on the mountain by the sea when he gave his revolutionary sermon.

Near my model of the X-1 stands a cross. Both of these "X's", both symbols, remind me daily of the need for people like you and me to change perspectives if we hope to become genuine pack-lugging sojourners on the Extra Mile. Whatever the barrier of sound or attitude, it must be repeatedly shattered if we are to burst beyond the mundane into the realm of the extraordinary as part of our newly minted lifestyle.

It worked 20 centuries ago. We have reason to believe it still works today. Who says? Jesus says. Simon says. Pass the secret along, fellow traveler; pass it on far and wide.

Two miles are always better than one.

MILE 2

Chapter 4: Extra-Milers Do More than Double the First Mile

"And if anyone gives even a cup of cold water to one
of these little ones because he is my disciple, I tell
you the truth, he will certainly not lose his reward."

~ Jesus

Secret # 4

The first mile is an obligation, the minimum. It is service without a smile, a kiss without affection, paying taxes but never bothering to vote. It is room temperature water, or worse, what was hauled out of the well the day before and left out in the desert sun.

Do we in modern day have any idea how hard it was to find cold refreshing water in the ancient Middle East of Jesus' era? There were certainly no ice cubes and almost no cool water. The daytime heat could be oppressive, especially when the sun was high overhead. At such times thirsty travelers were fortunate to get a few gulps of tepid, lukewarm water. Innkeepers didn't pay much attention to the niceties of room service. They weren't going to go out of their way to lower the water's temperature for the sake of an unknown pilgrim who most likely wouldn't pass that way again.

Water was a marketable commodity, even in the first century. It didn't come packaged or in plastic bottles with built-in spouts and added flavoring. It wasn't imported from France or Italy with the intention of selling it at high-end stores or in the best restaurants. Most people were glad to get a gulp of any non-toxic liquid that promised to keep them from dying of thirst. People would kill their neighbor or go to war over ordinary water rights. So a jar of cold, refreshing water was the stuff of which dreams were made.

The Old Testament tells of a battle when King David developed a craving for water from a particular well near his hometown. He apparently muttered longingly under his breath about how grand it would be to slake his considerable thirst with water from the cool, limpid spring located at the edge of his native village of Bethlehem. Three of David's top warriors overheard their general's whispered aside, spoken to no one in particular. But in their minds their leader's mere wish was their clear command.

In response to his hushed statement, they broke through the lines, filled a jug with cool water from the well at Bethlehem and, at risk of their own lives, brought its contents back to their king. David was so moved by the gesture that he poured the water onto the ground as a gift for God. He didn't drink a drop. He remarked that his three valiant men had put themselves in peril to honor him with a jug of his favorite water. He felt required to in turn salute them by passing on the water as a sacrifice to One higher than himself. The cold water from Bethlehem's well thus was swallowed up, consumed by the parched earth of the battlefield, a fitting tribute to David's trio of Extra Mile warriors.

Jesus also spoke of cold water, not for himself, but for others. In his economy there was no reward for room temperature, lukewarm or tepid water. In the hot, desert country of Palestine the kudos were reserved only for those who served with distinction, who went the Extra Mile, who produced at least a spring-fed chilled thirst-quencher in their pre-ice cube age.

His precept lives on. When people make known their thirst to us, we should dip deep into our figurative wells to supply their need – and more than just their need. Our response shouldn't come from a hot pool or the day-old cup sitting on a fly-populated table. A special trip to the water source is called for, even if it requires walking an Extra Mile to do so.

We hear the Rabbi say: "Let down the bucket for the one you serve. Deliver the pristine drink with panache. Accolades go exclusively to those who deliberately live on the Extra Mile road, that unique fraternity-sorority of cold-water givers who go far beyond the norm to serve those in their care."

Two cups of mere room-temperature water fail to equal one cup of really cold mountain-stream water. Doubling mediocrity misses the mark. Traveling two single miles, each traversed with both a knapsack and a chip on one's shoulder, come up short of the goal. Twice as much of anything, delivered in a lackadaisical manner, doesn't add up to one of something special presented with flair and fervor. Staying two nights at a two-star hotel is not equivalent to one night at a four-star hotel.

My wife and I were eating al fresco at our favorite local restaurant. We were seated by the valet stand, which allowed us to overhear the unguarded comments of the professional car-parkers. Some of the drivers would fetch a car, barely open the door for the owner, grab the extended tip, grunt an unintelligible thank you, slam the door, and then race away in search of another tip.

However, we noticed that one young man had a standout style. His attitude more than doubled what his fellow valets were doing. He courteously opened the door for the passenger, then ran around and did the same for the driver. He smiled, looked customers in the eyes, and accepted the proffered tip with genuine gratitude and a slight nod of the head, enunciating his appreciation by way of both words and body language. His cheery wave at the departing car provided a classy finale to an evening of fine dining.

We watched as an elderly couple got into their car. The cheerful valet went through his Extra Mile routine. But they had a special problem. How, they wanted to know, could they get to the westbound interstate entrance? They had no GPS. Their hearing was poor, which added to the confusion. We listened to the attendant as he patiently explained the various twists and turns, the rights and lefts, to the main highway. But the older folks couldn't seem to grasp the nuances of his instructions.

Without a trace of impatience, the valet offered to go get his own car and drive them to the interstate entrance, which he then proceeded to do. A few minutes later he returned, an even larger second tip in hand. He had demonstrated that cold water is many times more likely to be recognized and rewarded than tap water. The Extra Mile is more than doubling the first one. A genuine smile tops a grunt anytime.

Why is this principle difficult for some people to grasp? Perhaps it is because of the sheer simplicity of the precept. We are attracted to machines with many moving parts, which tend to contribute little to productivity while increasing the potential for a breakdown of some sort. Our fascination is with the complex. Conventional wisdom seems to favor bells-and-whistles over precision and simplicity.

This credo isn't really all that complicated: Go two miles, not one. Do it often and always. That's it.

But we prefer the palace to the manger for a birthplace. An Extra Mile and a cup of cold water seemingly have little relevance when it comes to customer service, enhancing a marriage, or improving the world. The boilerplate template from yet another seminar is preferable to simple kindness and common sense, which is becoming less and less common all the time.

When my wife and I moved to a new home, I decided to give myself a sabbatical from mowing the lawn. So who was to do the job? Serendipitously, at that very time a cheaply printed business card was placed under our front door's welcome mat, with an invitation to "call Antonio" for an estimate on lawn service. How timely, I thought.

So, I dialed the printed number and was graced with a recorded message, albeit in somewhat broken English. I must readily confess that the odds that I would have given for Antonio to actually return my call were nil to none. My inclination was to write him off and look for another lawn service.

But my bias was quickly proven to be as incorrect as it was prejudiced. Not only did Antonio call back that very evening, but he also came by to demonstrate his considerable mowing and gardening skills the next day, at precisely the time he had promised.

Antonio maintained our yard for many years and if I could have convinced him to move to the east coast with me, he would still be mowing my lawn to this day. Without hesitation, I recommended him to all of my friends. No one ever came back to me with anything but the highest praise for Antonio's work.

What was so special about Antonio? He was an Extra Mile guy. He went over and beyond the call of duty every time he cranked up his shiny lawn mower. If I called Antonio to help me on Tuesday instead of Wednesday because guests were coming over, he always did his best to accommodate. It's no wonder that in a matter of a few short years he hired extra employees, bought additional equipment, moved his family to a better neighborhood, and is now living the American dream.

Though he continued to speak with an accent, this was to both Antonio and me proof that he could do business in one more language than most of his competitors. Perhaps of greater significance, Antonio's main language was the unspoken one. It was the dialect of the Extra Mile, the international lingua franca of every era and culture, from Antonio's native village of Aguas Calientes (which ironically means Hot Water) to his brand-new home in the suburbs of Chicago.

Antonio learned that the Extra Mile is more than just doubling the first mile. There were many lawn services in my town. Indeed, I had tried a couple of them out before Antonio left his dog-eared card on my doorstep. What made the diminutive Mexican man who became my friend a standout was wrapped up in the extras. The additional attention to trimming the grass, blowing off the sidewalk, and doing it all with an infectious smile is what caused me to call Antonio back again and again.

This paradigm is not limited to my experience with Antonio. On multiple occasions I have been afforded ordinary, entry-level courtesies. These have all long since faded from my memory. They've been dumped into the vast indistinguishable trash barrel containing the mundane. No one remembers the first mile, even if it is done repeatedly. The experiences embedded in my memory are the really bad ones – and the truly lavish ones. I'm going to hazard a guess that it's the same for you, too. The ordinary is so, well, ordinary that it doesn't even register in our memory banks.

Being bumped from a flight, without the offer of compensation or any further help, tends to stick in one's mind. So, for different reasons, does being unexpectedly bumped up to first class. But multiple predictable flights sitting in coach, even when accompanied by a small beverage and a tiny bag of pretzels, somehow blend together.

Nothing special, though oft repeated, adds up to nothing memorable.

Average meanders into the vast reservoir of mediocrity. It takes the additional Extra Mile, the one featuring tinkling ice cubes in a world of room-temperature water, to create a lasting memory. It requires being an exceptional parking valet or a remarkable gardener to find a place on the A-Team. An endless series of ho-hum events will rarely forge the deep furrows in the brain that are required to create an unforgettably pleasant experience.

So, fellow travelers on the Extra Mile road, let us issue the clarion call to do more than merely double the first mile. Average blends into the woodwork. Normal is the sworn enemy of success. Adequate never takes the day.

Carpe diem. Otherwise, traveling companions, it is just another uneventful "diem" on the one-mile road to oblivion, that stretch of highway no one seems to remember, unpunctuated by memorable and refreshing water fountains. From Hot Water to Cool Water is at least two miles. Antonio found the way out of his town of "Hot Water" and, I daresay, so can you and I.

Let's keep traveling.

Chapter 5: Extra-Milers Leave Footprints of Authentic Gratitude

"Were not all ten cleansed?
Where are the other nine?"
~ Jesus

Secret # 5

Jesus was not easily impressed or surprised. Dealing with disease, demons, disasters, and even death were all part of a typical day's assignment. It took a lot to amaze the Rabbi whom even his enemies called Teacher, and his friends called Master. Yet, the record shows that on at least one occasion he was taken aback by, of all things, a spate of ingratitude.

It happened like this. Jesus was on the road that meandered between Galilee and Samaria. Along the way he encountered ten lepers who, by reason of their affliction, had been disenfranchised from society. At that time it was an entrenched belief that leprosy came upon those thus afflicted because of sinful behavior. It was also widely held that the disease was highly contagious. Hence, the appearance of the telltale spots on human skin required the disappearance of the spot-bearer from all communal activity. Lepers were banished from society to lurk in the shadows until they were declared cured, which might be never.

The lone relief to their perpetual loneliness was that lepers were allowed to associate with fellow lepers, on the assumption that they couldn't do each other much further harm. For this reason St. Luke's account details that there were ten lepers in the group Jesus encountered, a little colony hallmarked by agony and rejection. They were brought together out of the instinct for survival, rather than any real hope for revival.

Somehow the word spread to the leper colony that a healer was coming their way. So these ten lepers, nine Jews and a lone Samaritan, gathered on a mound overlooking the parade route. At the first sight of Jesus they commenced to chant hoarsely in unison. They engaged in this form of teamwork because the leprosy had damaged their vocal cords to the extent that they could only manage to croak. However, they reasoned that ten croaks might just add up to one halfway decent shout. So on the count of three, they united their raspy voices into a frog-like chorus.

Their intended goal was realized because the record shows that Jesus heard them. He then stopped the procession. He inspected the motley band. He said a few words. Then Jesus perfunctorily ordered them to go show themselves to the local priest, the equivalent of a modern doctor.

Not waiting to see their spots disappear, the ten shuffled off obediently, having been inspired by Jesus to exercise their faith.

Along the way, even as they went, they were all "cleansed" (a term that refers to physical restoration).

It is important to factor into the story that Samaritans were a despised caste in that era. In fact, the only way the lone Samaritan leper had been allowed to join the nine higher-class Jewish lepers was by reason of the infirmity that both ostracized all of them from others and united them to each other. However, once healed the Jewish nine took off for their homes in their "more important" part of town, leaving the Samaritan as the odd man out once more.

Then something strange occurred. Ironically, only the Samaritan, who had now been blackballed from the earlier Leper's Club, returned to thank Jesus. Have you noticed that we are frequently united in a crisis, only to return to our original prejudices when the sirens cease to wail and the storm is over? So, no longer having to abide by the rules of the disbanded group, the Samaritan decided to loop back and express personal heartfelt thanks to the Rabbi. In a loud voice, his newly strengthened vocal cords being used to proclaim his gratitude, he unashamedly and publicly made known to one and all the identity of the person who was the reason for his improved condition.

Two things immediately amazed Jesus: The single Samaritan's good manners and the ingratitude of the nine Jewish lepers. "Where are the other nine," asked Jesus. Where, indeed? No one seemed to have an answer; not that day, not any day.

The countless unwritten thank you notes of life beg an explanation, though one is seldom forthcoming. Why can voices be united in the midnight shadows of pain and disbanded in midday sun of gain? Do we only bond when in the emergency rooms of life?

Ironically, it was then that Jesus pronounced the Samaritan ex-leper "well", a powerful word that denotes complete healing; an additional bonus beyond the miraculous facelift granted the chorus of croakers an hour before. Unlike the ungrateful nine, the tenth, the appreciative leper, was granted more than a dermatological miracle. He was healed inside and out. His cure was more than skin deep.

The thankful Samaritan, who had walked back the Extra Mile to say thanks, was given an additional benefit, which the other nine in their haste failed to receive. He was set free from his self-centeredness, the attitude that, if unaddressed, would thereafter grant him with a child's smooth skin externally, but a diseased and childish (rather than childlike) heart.

What happened to the other nine? Who knows? They may have used their refurbished vocal cords to tout their own praises. They probably used their creamy new skins to attract admiring girls. They likely retold the story of the parade that stopped for them countless times, ever editing it to make themselves the grand marshals of the event, giving the Rabbi a mere supporting role. Such is the faulty, egocentric memory of the One-Miler.

Ingratitude does strange things to a person. A spirit of entitlement red-pencils history. It keeps the thankless nine perpetually within the first mile zone, where nothing of significance happens to or through them. "He healed me, helped me, gave me a hand when I was down and out; so what?" is the mantra of the ungrateful. This is the motto of the thankless; the creed of the self-absorbed.

Sadly, such cases of petty ingratitude are not limited to the first century. Consider the case of Edmund Spencer, who was standing on the beach at Evanston, Illinois on September 8, 1860 when the passenger ferry Lady Elgin started to sink. He saw a woman going down amidst the breakers. Shedding his clothes he unselfishly plunged into the chilly waters of Lake Michigan. He swam to quickly save the frantic woman.

Then Spencer heard another person shouting out for help. Again, he risked his own safety for a stranger's survival. This occurred repeatedly, until the valiant swimmer collapsed in the sand, unable to move. Edmund Spencer successfully put his life on the line for 17 people that day. He saved them all. However, he never fully regained his health. The stress of that day did him in. He was never the same again.

When he was 81 years old, Spencer died in California, far from the Midwest beach where he had become a reluctant hero. His obituary mentioned his bravery on that September afternoon. The brief news report also added this sad indictment: Not one of the 17 people he saved ever returned to thank him!

Alas, my fellow pilgrims, the experience of Jesus and the nine self-centered lepers was not an isolated one. Ingratitude still is, like leprosy once was, an epidemic. And the widespread attitude of ingratitude invariably will keep you and me lepers on the inside, whatever may be our apparent winsomeness or beauty outwardly.

Silence will never make us "well". Our thanksgiving is ordained to be shouted aloud atop the same mound from which we placed our original desperate croaking request. This leads us to ask anew: "Where are the other nine?"

Perhaps we can find them by collectively asking ourselves a few probing questions...

Have we stopped recently to meaningfully thank our mentors, the men or women who have diligently pulled us behind them to where we are today?

Is Father's Day or Mother's Day the only time we pause to show gratitude to our parents, rough-hewn though their efforts may seem to be or have been?

When did we last write to one of our former schoolteachers, to say thanks for showing us how to read, to communicate, and to succeed?

How about the coaches who, in spite of their seeming toughness, instilled in us life lessons we still draw upon daily? Have they heard our cry of thanks? Let's search for them diligently and let them hear the magic words: "Thank you".

Then there's the pastor, the rabbi, or the priest who quietly served our family over the years. Does such faithfulness count enough to merit an overdue call or an email, celebrating years of obscurity, during which the reverend's name was kept out of the newspaper for all the right reasons?

Do we want to surprise a group who boasts that they've seen it all? Then stop by the police station, not to complain about the neighborhood hoodlums, but to express admiration and appreciation to those who risk their lives daily on our behalf.

Do we love our country? Let's fly the flag, stop complaining about everything we don't like, and place flowers on an unknown veteran's grave. "God bless America" is a weak, shallow request invoked blithely to the Almighty if it is not generously sprinkled with gratitude.

Is genuine romance waning in our lives? How about some appreciation for the spouse we once loved dearly, the life-mate we even liked? And let's try to express our gratitude in such a way as not to add insult to injury. (Translation: No small appliances for the ladies, or ties for the men!)

The kids have heard enough about their lackluster grades and messy rooms already. Is there something affirming we can find to say by way of thanks to our children?

Finally, how about God? A simple prayer of thanks from deep within the heart would do nicely, uttered from now on more meaningfully and more often than in the past.

I said earlier that I had a few questions for those of us on this journey. I just counted the questions and found, coincidentally, that there are nine of them.

Maybe in answering these inquiries together we may have, after so many centuries, finally found our missing lepers. They weren't a mile outside of ancient Jericho after all. They are in Miami, Peoria, Jackson, La Jolla, Vancouver, Manchester, Toronto, London, and Aberdeen.

They are "we".

And now, like all newly determined people of the Extra Mile, we're on the road that loops back to someone or something long forgotten. We are returning from whence we came to shout a message that it is never too late to herald: Thanks! The additional mile will be worth it, both to us and to those who need to hear our words of gratitude.

So, let's backtrack together, Extra Mile companions. And on the way, allow me to say it yet again: Many thanks for the company. One can be a lonely number on this Extra Mile road, as all "well" Samaritan ex-lepers know.

Chapter 6: Extra-Milers Walk Resolutely

"...Jesus resolutely set out for Jerusalem."
~ St. Luke

Secret # 6

Resolute. Now there's a word filled with passion and forged like steel. It is onomatopoeic. It hints of granite, grit, and an unyielding grip. I speak the word and simultaneously see a lean, tanned rock climber, fingers like talons, slowly ascending a sheer mountain face. I envision a lonely runner; three years removed from the next Olympiad, putting in one more lap before sunset, visions of gold on her mind.

Resolute. The "t" is like an unexpected bump in the road. It forms a lower case cross. The sudden gutturalness it produces when pronounced is out of place, at least in the environment of the preceding silky syllables.

And that's what makes it a remarkable word. Resolute suggests triumph over the struggles of life. It is a word for champions. It refers to that place where the mundane suddenly encounters the unexpected demands of servant leadership; when the rough stuff intrudes upon our placidity and calls for tough decisions and tenacious follow-through.

Perhaps that's why all but three American presidents since Rutherford B. Hayes have chosen to work at a desk made from the timbers of the HMS Resolute. There are more practical and equally historical worktables. Until the 1850s the HMS Resolute plied the oceans, especially above the rim of the frigid Arctic Circle. Today this heavy presidential desk is still the choice of Democrats and Republicans alike. It perennially remains in the Oval Office due to the fitting name of the ship from whose side it was taken. Resolute is a word suited to both the challenges of the high seas and the demands of high office.

Jesus resolutely set out for Jerusalem. Why was such determination needed for this particular trip? When he had walked the miles from Galilee to Judea in the past, he had often sauntered. Most of the time he seemed to welcome, even relish, interruptions along the way. He was ever open to side-trips, the detours leading to the bedside of a sick woman or to bless a shy child. Jesus had no apparent need for either an agenda or a watch. Even Hollywood, in its typically uninspiring celluloid interpretations of Jesus' early ministry, invariably show him and his band of disciples moving in slow motion, as though trying to figure out what to do next. The motley group appears to be in search of a mission rather than resolutely implementing one.

Then suddenly Jesus seems to have found his compass. He has new direction and drive. The literal translation says that at this juncture "he set his face with steadfastness." Now and henceforth his eyes, like those of a lion fixed on a grazing gazelle, refuse to dart. The coordinates for his future are locked on and sealed up. Jerusalem has become to him the personification of both cross and cross hairs. The target is fixed. It will never be out of his direct line of vision again. Ever. The hour has come. He is resolute and will hereafter behave with resolution.

Was Jesus' midcourse transformation actually so abrupt and defining? I think not. He was never adrift on the inside, however casual his outward behavior may have seemed. His moniker was Master, precisely because he knew his destiny. Jesus knew where he was headed, even while appearing to just mosey along. His life was in a deliberate holding pattern, awaiting the command from his Father to fulfill the miracle of the ages.

Yet, according to St. Luke's account, something occurred at this point, something that gave Jesus a more concentrated focus. Hereafter he would bypass the towns where previously he might have stopped for a cup of water or a meal. He perfunctorily told all would-be disciples that no one who puts a hand to the plow and turns back should expect to be his follower. The "new Jesus" was more demanding and determined. He was resolute and wanted all comers to be resolute as well. He was going to Jerusalem. His new mantra was lead, follow, or get out of the way.

On our own Extra Mile journey toward our personal Jerusalem our focus, our resolution, is equally necessary.

We know scientifically that there is a big difference between a flashlight and a laser beam. The flashlight's widespread rays have certain benefits, but not if concentrated power and energy are required. A flashlight is adequate enough for illuminating a dark path, but its diffused rays cannot cut through metal or be used in surgery. A laser is needed to cut steel.

Resolution is intense, almost obsessive. By contrast we live in an age enamored with fragmentary ideas. We can't seem to concentrate. Attention Deficit Syndrome is a real problem, and a figurative one, too. Every morning many millions rise from a fitful night's pseudo-rest to saddle the bronco of schedule, only to then ride haphazardly in 40 directions until sunset. Too many people are like owls, ever turning and blinking, phobic that something may be missed while the sands of time slip away. We dabble and divide when we should be resolute and conquer. In the process it wears us out and makes us question our destiny.

A farmer got up early to plow the acreage down by the creek. He noted that the tractor was low on fuel, so he went to the shed for gasoline. As he walked toward the barn he glanced to the left and saw that the fence needed repair. So he stopped to fix it. Then the chickens started clucking hungrily. He left the dilapidated fence in favor of feeding his clamoring fowl. The entire day found the increasingly distracted farmer rushing from one unfinished task to another. Nightfall arrived and the lower 40 acres by the creek had yet to feel the sharp edges of his unused plow.

When his wife casually asked him over supper about the nature of his day, the normally laidback farmer responded with irritation. His frustration at his lack of accomplishment, while understandable, was avoidable. He correctly blamed himself. He had allowed himself to become distracted – again. At least he was honest. Whether he'll repeat the same mistake in the future depends on whether or not he becomes more focused, more resolute.

The rub manifests itself because Extra-Milers tend to be servant leaders. It is a challenge to be resolute when, at a moment's notice, you may be asked to tote a knapsack or fetch a cup of cold water. The One-Miler's nemesis is doing too little or not doing the right thing, whereas the Extra-Miler attempts too much and can thereby get off track. The former tends to rust out, while the latter is prone to burn out.

Ringing phones, unanswered emails, tweets, exasperated customers, a pleading child, a hurting parishioner or a bereaved friend, the demanding boss or neglected spouse, numerous needy employees – they all beg us for a piece of our calendar and our checkbook. Who will be the ones to hear us say no, wait, later, tomorrow? The hard-nosed boss usually won't wait (though perhaps he should), whereas the pleading child shouldn't wait (but probably will). What are we to do?

The answer has been discovered by seasoned Extra-Milers who have learned to carry only one soldier's pack at a time, to travel one road at a time, to serve one person at a time. We are called to learn from the best. He says: "Set your face toward Jerusalem. Make sure your destination is true. Then, be resolute."

I watched an attendant at the information booth of a large mall near Chicago. It was during the last days of the Christmas season. Clamoring shoppers, who had long since lost the spirit of the holidays, surrounded her cubicle like snarling wild beasts. They barked staccato questions: "Where? Why? When? Who? How?" Their body language was tense, their voices terse. But the attendant stayed amazingly calm through the ordeal, taking care of one entreaty and demand after another, never allowing herself to become flustered.

Though I was quite busy myself, her kindness and focus so intrigued me that I stopped to observe this phenomenon. When there was an unexpected lull I approached the service desk. I told the lady that I'd been watching her handle one tough situation after another, with control and aplomb. My question was not where to find a department store or to inquire about a misplaced package. No, I just wanted to know how she operated with such graciousness amidst the feeding frenzy of the holiday sharks.

She looked me straight in the eye. I'll never forget her total concentration. A Mona Lisa-like smile played on the edges of her lips. The impatient let-me-check-my-watch-again shopper, who had rushed up on her left, didn't seem to register on her radar screen. It was as though she and I had sat just down in a walled garden for midafternoon tea and scones. In her mind, only I existed for that brief but unhurried moment.

On hearing my question she smiled broadly and said softly: "Well, sir, I simply take care of one person, one problem, at a time. I give the individual I'm currently assisting my full attention. For example when I've dealt fully with you, I'll move on to this lady, then the next person, and so on." (This she said, ever so slightly gesturing at the finger-drumming shopper to her left.) After I walked away I looked back and, sure enough, she was totally absorbed with helping the finger-tapper. Another couple was now impatiently waiting in line behind her, but the info lady politely motioned for them to hold tight, she'd help them next. She had found the secret of the Extra Mile servant: Help one centurion at a time. Be resolute. Love the one you're with.

To be intensely focused may seem impossible when it comes to a task involving service. After all, the squeaky wheel gets the oil. So, is it not more prudent to give in to the demands of the harried customer who shouts loudest? Shouldn't the farmer leave his inanimate broken fence for the lively clucking chickens? When should we drop the backpack of the soldier we are serving in favor of another's baggage, especially if the second soldier outranks the first? Should we not give in to the loudest, the richest, or the most demanding voice?

All of these are valid questions. But didn't Jesus tell the story of a shepherd who left 99 sheep to search for a single lost lamb? The 99 sheep surely made more noise than the lone lamb that was in peril. But the number of bleats per second was not the telling factor in whether the shepherd would choose to aid the large flock or the lone stray. He was attuned to need, not as mandated by a choir of noisy ewes, but based on his predetermined priorities as a servant-leader. Because the shepherd knew what was important he couldn't be pushed into conformity by a prevailing majority opinion, even if the vote was 99 to 1.

Some Extra Mile decisions are uncomplicated. The firehouse siren goes off in a mid-American hamlet. Does a volunteer firefighter finish mowing the lawn (as he had promised his wife he would do), or does he drop everything and join his fellows to extinguish the life-imperiling blaze? The answer is simple. One must always go with the choice that has the most enduring value. The lawn can wait. The burning home containing a trapped infant cannot. When two goals are in conflict, the one with the most to commend it, in reference to time and eternity, should prevail.

Jesus told a parable that has become a classic, about the so-called Good Samaritan. (We'll deal with this more fully in the next chapter.) The story is about a man on a journey who was set upon by thieves. They beat and robbed him. Shortly thereafter two ministers, whose job it was to care for the needy, passed by the injured man in favor of getting to church on time. Then came the infidel, the one most people thought knew or cared little about spiritual matters. However, unlike the speeding so-called spiritual men on their way to church, the Samaritan stopped, took the injured man to the hospital, and even offered to pay the portion of the doctor's bill not covered by insurance. Who, asked Jesus, was on task? Who was truly resolute? When the reluctant answer came back, "the Samaritan", all that Jesus said was, "Go and do likewise." But not all Extra Mile choices are so clearly spelled out, are they? Principles for making good decisions must be first framed, and then taught. Common sense must inform our focus and resolve.

For example, the other day I was at a store checkout counter. The cash register attendant was stocking the shelves behind her. Though she saw me, she continued to fill the empty bins, effectively ignoring me. When I politely asked her to take a short break and help me, you would have thought I had interrupted a meeting of the National Security Council during a nuclear crisis. Couldn't I see she had an important job to do? How dare I interrupt her crucial mission? After all, I was just a customer making a purchase, whereas the pressing inventory needed immediate attention (at least in her mind).

The lady was resolute and focused, but on the wrong thing. Empty bins are there because shoppers have shopped. If the attendant doesn't soon learn to view the person standing at her register as far more important than the bins begging to be restocked, the bins will be empty at the store down the street, the one with the superior customer service. Then the newly unemployed cashier will blame the economy, the government, anyone but herself for the fallout caused by her misplaced priorities and fuzzy focus. Bins can be restocked after hours. Customers need attention now!

So, let's walk with resolve. Let's stay on task and remember that the Extra Mile only counts if we, the pack-carriers, are on the right track. Let's avoid the winding paths that, though long, tend to lead us away from our mission. Serve one centurion at a time, and serve him or her exceedingly well.

Let's be resolute to the end – the end that bears dividends.

MILE 2

Chapter 7: Extra-Milers Are Good Samaritans

"Which of these three do you think was neighbor to
the man who fell into the hands of robbers?" The
expert in the law replied, "The one who had mercy
on him."
Jesus told him, "Go and do likewise."
~ Jesus when conversing with a tricky lawyer

Secret # 7

In the Palestine of Jesus' era, "good Samaritan" was an
oxymoron. The two words, "good" and "Samaritan", didn't
belong in the same sentence, much less side by side. The
Samaritans were hated and scorned. They were considered
anything but good. They were universally viewed with contempt
as half-breeds, a mixed race that was born from the co-mingling
of Jewish and Gentile blood many centuries earlier. Thus, the
Samaritans were like the fabled Civil War soldier who wore gray
trousers and a blue shirt, only to be shot at from both sides.

Samaritans couldn't win for losing. They didn't get respect at any level – not from Jews, not from Gentiles.

So, the hated Samaritans had created their own little closed society; an enclave that was ingrown and exclusive out of necessity. They had migrated to a remote mountain and built a downsized version of Herod's prestigious Temple in Jerusalem to serve as their wannabe house of worship. Samaritan rituals were thinly veiled imitations of the practices of Judaism. Their every move was a subconscious mimicry of their more sophisticated relatives; a plea for the acceptance and respect that was never quite within their grasp. They were pariahs, outcasts, nobodies.

Despite their best efforts, the counterfeit religious practices of the Samaritans gained them no respectability. The harder they tried, the more they were scorned. Their attempts at piety garnered the muffled laughter of pranksters, and probably provided fodder for the routines of ancient Jewish comedians. ("Seriously though, folks, I was going through Samaria the other day and...") "Samaritan jokes" were probably all the rage during the first century.

But as usual Jesus turned the tables on conventional wisdom. He did so in the form of a parable, which is a pithy story with a spiritual meaning. Ancient parables were so engaging and mysterious that they often mesmerized the listeners. Parables tended to creep up behind the audience and suddenly shout "boo!" Just when you thought you had the point, the point had you.

In the era before television and cinema, storytelling was wonderful entertainment. Jesus was widely considered to be a first-rate storyteller. Whenever he would gather a group around him and casually say "once upon a time", the lucky listeners would move in close, huddle up and lean forward. They were in for a verbal blockbuster. The Rabbi's parables added color to their black-and-white world.

Jesus had a way of putting the most difficult concepts into understandable word pictures. Sometimes the parables seemed to come out of the blue. On other occasions they were crafted as a response to an inane question or a caustic remark. This particular account was spun from a lawyer's legal sparring with the Master Wordsmith.

Well, to be fair, the text suggests that it was really much more than a little lexical jousting. The sly attorney was doing his best to trick Jesus. This unnamed expert in religious law saw Jesus as a Galilean country bumpkin; little more than a whetting stone upon whom he could sharpen his Ivy League-trained courtroom skills. But it was a serious underestimation, and a bad move on the haughty lawyer's part.

At first Jesus, with a twinkle in his eye, played along. The lawyer asked his leading question: "What is necessary to inherit eternal life?" Jesus answered the original question with one of his own, a disarming form of debate, intended not to derail, but to enrich the argument. It was a cultural way of disarming the strident aspects of controversy.

So now let's imagine Jesus, first stroking his beard, then squinting, and finally saying slowly in Aramaic: "So, you want to know what a person must do to inherit eternal life? Good, good. Well, you're the lawyer, right? Summa cum laude graduate no doubt? Isn't this your area of expertise? I'm a lowly rabbi. I'd be interested in what you think as an attorney-at-law."

The barrister mumbled something from the Torah about loving God fully, and loving your neighbor as much as one's self. Little did he know, as the words dribbled from his lips that he had already lost the case. But for the moment Jesus probably just nodded approvingly at his reply, and said: "Not bad, young fellow. You get an A+. Flesh out your most excellent answer a bit more and you'll go far." With that, Jesus turned to go.

It was only then that the counselor realized he'd been outwitted. He had allowed the defendant to become the prosecutor. To redeem himself before all of the potential clients that surrounded him, he dug himself in deeper by asking a further question, one to which he did not know the answer. "And who is my neighbor?" he stammered, red-faced, trying to stall until he could think of something wittier to say.

Good lawyers never knowingly ask a question to which they don't already know the answer. This is taught to all aspiring attorneys in Law 101. Jesus turned back with a smile playing on his face. "Once upon a time..." he began. The trap was sprung before the story was told. And it was, by all accounts, a humdinger of a parable – replete with robbers, villains, a victim, and an unlikely champion.

As the story began Jesus introduced an unnamed stooge who had been a victim of a violent robbery. A couple of apathetic ministers, a bloodthirsty gang of marauding thugs, and an innkeeper rounded out the supporting cast. On Jesus' verbal stage the two ministers and a cabal of thieves quickly made their entrances and exits, leaving the floor to the leading actor who makes his appearance rather late in the story. The star of the show has long been known as the "Good Samaritan" (though Jesus never actually referred to him as good).

The tale went like this. A man was on a journey when he was assaulted, robbed, and then bludgeoned for good measure. Two religious leaders saw him groaning by the roadside but chose to ignore his cries for help. On this cue the Samaritan merchant entered. He had every reason to leave the injured Jewish man wallowing in his own blood. After all, the Jews had mistreated his people for centuries. By contrast and to the contrary, he behaved with exceptional grace. He took the injured man to a nearby hotel, personally attended to his wounds, and even left enough money with the proprietor so that the victim could receive follow-up medical help in the days to come.

The early departure of the two hard-hearted ministers from the stage leaves us, the modern audience, with a sense of disappointment. We wonder how these reverends could have been so heartless. The thieves failed by reason of bad proactive behavior, but the priests failed because of wrong reactive behavior. The thieves were crooks, but the ministers were care-less. The churchgoers responded to the urgent (get to church on time) rather than the important (see and attend to real human needs).

So, as the parable concludes we are left with just three actors on the stage of this ancient play: A bloody man at death's door, a despised foreign traveler, and a yawning hotel manager. Some believe the prototype for the foreign traveler on the journey, the "good" Samaritan, was Jesus himself. Wasn't he ever the outcast rabbi, touching lepers when others wouldn't even get near them, consorting with taxmen and bad women alike? The people his contemporaries tiptoed around and avoided, Jesus encircled and embraced. Prejudice never colored Jesus' responses though many mocked him for it.

Jesus lived in the shadow of perpetual xenophobia. He was a Jew, sure enough, but he loved outsiders, really loved them. And he encouraged others to do the same. Yet, not many bought in to his philosophy, least of all the leaders of his day.

It wasn't kosher, don't you know, hobnobbing with vagrants and vagabonds, not to mention a beat-up, bloodied tourist. Who knows? Maybe the victim had invited the wrath of God upon himself by reason of some secret sin in his life. The thieves may have been divine tools opined some. Wouldn't it be unwise to interfere by offering first aid to a man under the judgment of God? Don't get in the way of Adonai. Let God do his work. Thus the two apathetic preachers were bonafide heroes to a significant segment of the crowd. It seems that even those with hearts chiseled from hard granite have groupies.

Ah, but the Samaritan pilgrim, who later generations would label "good", went over and beyond the call of duty. The law requiring that service be rendered to an injured Israelite did not bind him legally. He was a Samaritan, not a Jew. But what the law could not do out of compulsion, love did out of compassion.

Who could have blamed him, the target of many a pejorative jibe, had he mounted his burro and trotted off into the sunset? However, this stranger with no calling card or ID beyond his inherent goodness, allowed a self-proclaimed enemy to lather his saddle with blood from injuries most likely received by the hands of his very own countrymen.

If you travel the winding road from Jerusalem to Jericho today you'll be invited to stop at a wayside house claiming to be this ancient inn. Be forewarned: Only in the tourist brochures is this considered to be the actual place. Yet, though merely a fabrication built by those still wishing to separate travelers from their money, albeit more legally these days, the quaint locale provides a picturesque setting to relive this powerful allegory.

The Samaritan was a better neighbor than Mister Rogers. (Remember Mister Rogers': "Won't you be my neighbor?") This Samaritan traversed the Extra Mile. He even left extra money to cover future hospice care for the injured. And he promised to pay any additional medical expenses upon his return to the area.

One-Milers are intent on accomplishing only their self-appointed assignments. The priority is seemingly to do the dynamic equivalent of getting to church on time. The man or woman in the ditch is quickly dismissed as an inconvenience. It is easy to look the other way, find a theological loophole, or simply leave it to Joe or Jane Samaritan. The urgent displaces the important.

Most of us think we don't have the time to be a good neighbor.

John Claypool relates the story of a seminary professor who recruited fifteen volunteers from his theology class for an experiment. When they met, at 2 o'clock one afternoon, he handed each of them sealed instructions.

Five of the envelopes instructed the recipients to walk across campus without delay. They were told not to loiter, lest their class grade be docked by reason of tardiness in carrying out their assignment. The educator called these five people the 'high hurry group'.

Another five were labeled the 'medium hurry group'. They were given 45 minutes to travel the same distance across campus. They were urged to move swiftly, but told not to rush unnecessarily.

The last five were given three hours to cross the campus. The 'low hurry group' could take it far easier than the others. Each group was told they would receive further instructions when they arrived at their destination.

Unbeknownst to any of the fifteen students, their professor had arranged for some drama majors to sit along the designated route and play out the roles of people in need. One person was wailing, apparently engulfed in grief. Another seemed to have suffered a seizure of some sort. A third was quite ill, retching in fact. You get the idea.

All of the ministerial students made their way along the same path. None of those who had been assigned serious time constraints stopped for anyone. Two of the medium hurry group helped someone. But virtually all of the low hurry people were responsive to one or more of the needy people.

The principle that emerges from this study is that time pressure can hinder moral judgment. We can be so rushed with our own sundry agendas that our willingness to respond to human need is compromised. No matter how lofty our idealism, the fact remains that when our calendar is filled to overflowing it shapes how we serve others.

Of course, we cannot stop to personally address every need along the road of life. Even Jesus limited his ministry. In his final prayer he gave thanks that he had finished all that had been given to him to do. But had every blind eye been opened in Jerusalem? Were there no lepers left for him to heal in Galilee? Were there no lame people hobbling about in Nazareth?

Actually we know that there were many sick and hurting folks that had never felt the touch of the Master's hand. Later we see Jesus' disciples ministering to the needs of those their Rabbi left untouched. Had he not said that there would always be an abundance of poor asking for alms and requiring help? The point was that he had done all of his own work and more. But the rest he left for others to do. He had gone the Extra Mile and those following in his footprints were expected to do the same.

George Buttrick said that asking the identity of one's neighbor is a condemnation. He added, "True neighborliness is not curious to know where the boundaries run; it cares as little for boundaries as sun and rain care for the contour lines upon our maps. It seeks not for limits, but for opportunities."

A final observation is in order. Thoroughly modern Samaritans may be inclined to hire someone to do the first aid; the fetching and the carrying; the dirty work. Isn't it possible to write a check instead of applying a tourniquet? Didn't the hero of Jesus' story hire the innkeeper to finish the work? Yes, indeed. But though we may be able to hire someone to do some of our work, we cannot pay a stand-in to do all of our work. At some point we must roll up our own sleeves and apply the bandages ourselves. We must get involved in the plight of humanity; get down in the ditch; cross the aisle; lend a hand.

Most of us have an unwritten contract with those we label neighbors that reads: "You scratch my back and I'll scratch yours. I'll lend you my lawnmower in the summer if you'll lend me your snow blower in the winter. I'll give you a dozen eggs today for a pound of sugar tomorrow."

But the marvel of this Samaritan is that he shared his time and resources without any promise of equal repayment. There was no quid pro quo, real or implied. Indeed, all that he got out of the deal was a used first aid kit, a tired donkey, empty pockets, and a messed-up schedule. Helping people is seldom neat and tidy. It is messy. The Samaritan learned that service is preceded by a willingness to be both interrupted and prevailed upon.

Service isn't a solitary or occasional action. It is a lifestyle.

If we learn to walk the Extra Mile we shouldn't expect accolades from the robbers or the "righteous". Our accolades will come in the form of a divine set of hands clapping on that grand and future day. However, those applauding hands will be the ones that really matter. It will be, for all pilgrims on the Extra Mile, the ovation that means the most.

Then redeemed Extra-Milers will hear the words: "Well done, my good and faithful servant ..." And the original "good" Samaritan will thank you and me for wisely using the two coins he left behind; for running an inn beside a dusty road; for providing aid for those who could not walk on their own. The aha moment at the story's end is this: The Samaritan is not us. It is him. It is Jesus, making a cameo appearance in his own story.

So, let's turn on the "vacancy" sign and make room for a few more road-weary, downtrodden travelers. We are merely the Master's hoteliers along the Extra Mile road. Extra-Milers are Good Samaritans.

Let's keep looking for those who may need a ride to the inn, the one where healing is possible and miracles still happen.

MILE 2

Chapter 8: Extra-Milers Genuinely Care About Others

"I tell you the truth, whatever you did for one of the
least of these brothers of mine, you did for me."
~ Jesus

Secret # 8

A few years ago I was board chairman of an organization
that invited former NBA great Bob Love to speak at its annual
banquet. During the meal that preceded Bob's presentation he
and I had a chance to get acquainted.

Bob shared openly with me about the stuttering problem
that had plagued him throughout his star-studded sports career.
It was quite a story, one I heard retold with fewer details in his
riveting after-dinner speech, during which only the slightest
vestiges of his former serious speech impediment surfaced.

How did he move from being a chronic stutterer to his new
role as a compelling motivational speaker? Bob grew up amidst
thirteen siblings in rural Louisiana. He developed his stuttering
problem by imitating a relative he admired who had a similar

problem. However, when the stammering became a permanent fixture, Bob chose to escape the taunts of his peers by imagining himself a famous basketball star.

Too poor to have a store-bought basketball hoop, Bob made one out of coat hangers, which he installed on the side of his grandmother's house. Often he practiced for hours daily on his backyard makeshift court. Gradually his seemingly impossible boyhood dream morphed into reality. After a stellar college stint at Southern University in Louisiana, where he attracted national attention, Bob (nicknamed "Butterbean") moved on to a pro career. He played for the Cincinnati Royals, the Milwaukee Bucks, and then for the Chicago Bulls.

While we were eating I asked Bob what it was like to try out for a pro team. He acted nonchalant, displaying genuine humility. "Oh," he said slowly, "at that level it isn't about the one who plays best, because everyone does. It's a matter of inner resolve and mental toughness. You must really want to excel or you'll soon be taking the Greyhound bus home. You have to be willing to go the Extra Mile."

Bob Love certainly went the Extra Mile for the Chicago team. For seven of his eight years with the Bulls he was the top scorer. During the same period he was thrice named an NBA All Star. In less than a decade Bob rocketed through the crowd of "ordinary" professional athletes into the rarified air of the upper tier, that of the enduring heroes. His name was destined to be written large and long in marble, not with chalk. He was one of the immortals.

And then he hurt his back. The storied statistics came to an abrupt halt. He found that the world had no place for an injured, stuttering former athlete. An operation on his spine led to the dismal prognosis that he would likely be partially paralyzed for life. Upon hearing that news his wife packed up, saying she couldn't face the prospect of a husband who was "both a stutterer and a cripple." With only a cane to lean on, Bob hit rock bottom.

The former star, once adulated by millions, found himself cleaning tables at a Seattle Nordstrom's for less than five dollars an hour. He told me that he'd often overhear customers whisper to each other: "Isn't that Bob Love? No way. Can't be. Love was a star. Must be a look-alike. That guy's a busboy." Even worse, every now and then he'd have to wait on a pro player he'd once beaten on the basketball court. But Bob told me that the ordeal only served to make him stronger and more determined to somehow overcome.

He decided, while waiting for lightning to strike, to become the best table cleaner in the world. He shared with me how he learned to wipe each table down perfectly. He attained his goal, which at the time was simply to reach the apex of the busboy profession. He was again the best at something, even if "something" was cleaning tables and washing dishes. While he was aware that no trophies would be awarded for this latest "victory", Bob felt like a winner for the first time in what seemed like an eternity.

Then lightning did strike. One of the company's owners offered to pay for him to undergo speech therapy. The net result was that a man, who couldn't give a post-game interview when he was a hotshot player because of his stammering, could finally complete a sentence without halting or stumbling.

Bob was subsequently offered the job of Community Relations Director for his former team, the Chicago Bulls. Ironically, his assignment was to communicate with hundreds of thousands of people every year. That's what he was doing the night I met him, giving an encouraging talk with his newly restored gift of speech. After I introduced him he proceeded to hold everyone captive for 20 minutes, whereupon he ended with these words: "Don't give up and always try to do your best. If you take the first step, someone will help you take the next one."

Now, as the imaginary applause following Bob's speech fades in our minds, please put his riveting story on hold for a few minutes. Let me tell you a parallel account, one equally powerful though hardly as well known.

Years ago I came to know a former NBA player, Mark. By his admission Mark wasn't ever on the A-Team. (In fact, the Chicago Bulls drafted him in the fourth round, one that no longer exists in the NBA.) Mark would certainly have excelled on any team of top-rank amateurs, but in the pros he registered just above the group clutching those one-way bus tickets back to their little towns and hamlets.

Indeed, though Mark made it through camp, he was cut after the pre-game season. His confidence badly shaken, Mark ended up trying out with the Portland Trailblazers. He started the season there, but knew he wasn't ever going to be a significant or enduring part of the team. To quote Mark, "I wasn't playing at all well; wasn't feeling good about myself. I was scared silly about my future and pretty much in denial that my days in the NBA were numbered."

Early in the season the Trailblazers went on their first Midwest road trip, which would include games at Milwaukee and Chicago. Mark was quite excited that he might have a chance to get some playtime in front of family and friends. In Milwaukee he was given significant time on the court. But at Chicago, where it really counted to him, it was a different story. The coach ordered him to sit, glued to the bench, while the clock ticked away.

With four minutes left in the Chicago game, with the Bulls trouncing the Blazers, the coach called Mark's number. Mark wasn't warmed up. By contrast, the Bulls players on the court were in the groove, playing well, especially Bob Love. However, the point was that Mark was finally in the game.

Mark had become acquainted with Bob Love during Mark's less-than-glorious stint with the Bulls. They had played opposite each other in practice so Mark knew the power and skill of his opponent. The chances for him to make a good showing in front of his family against Bob Love were negligible. Butterbean was good anytime, but he was in top form that night. Mark told me that he didn't stand a chance – and he knew it, too.

Mark has also told me more than once, at my request, about what happened over the next couple of minutes. It still gives me chills. Mark started out by running up and down the court with the flow of play. Suddenly, for reasons still unknown to him, the ball was in his hands. A few hesitant dribbles later and he was headed for the basket, having beaten all but one opponent, Bob Love.

Bob was matching Mark stride for stride. The thought came to Mark that he was about to be made to look like a fool at his only Chicago appearance in front of his family and friends. Time seemed to stand still. Mark could imagine the disappointment of his parents at his being blocked by Bob, though they would certainly understand considering Love's superior athleticism.

Even as Mark's mind raced through his limited options, he heard Bob say something to him almost under his breath. Amazingly, Bob didn't stutter when he spoke. Bob said to Mark, with nary a trace of a stammer, all the while running at his side: "Go ahead, Marco, shoot it!" With that, Bob ran ahead of Mark once they reached the foul line, making it look to the crowd that Mark had put a fake on him.

Having been given permission to do so by one of the NBA's star players, Mark took aim at the basket. What came next was one of the most miraculous (and little known) feats in the annals of the NBA. Mark drained the shot, to the everlasting awe of his family and friends, not to mention the fans. The place went wild. Even though the two points didn't mean much technically, considering the huge lead held by the Bulls, it was an emotional victory for Mark. David had defeated Goliath.

Mark told me he can think of only one motive for Bob Love's kindness to him. Most star players disdained mediocre rookies like him. But Bob was a gentleman who lived up to his last name – Love. He was willing to look weak for a moment, so that a lesser player could look strong. And for an instant, when it mattered most, Bob didn't stutter. Five silky-smooth words came streaming out of his mouth, in a stage whisper only Mark would hear: "Go ahead, Marco, shoot it." And now you have heard the whisper, too, the whisper kept secret for all of these years.

Extra-Milers are like that, aren't they? Jesus said that what we do to the least of these will be remembered. Years later, when Bob Love had only a cane to lean on, someone would help him learn to speak clearly, permanently. I suggest that his speech therapy began with five words: "Go ahead, Marco, shoot it."

Caring about others (or the opposite) always has a way of coming back to either help or haunt. The boomerang inevitably returns to the one who threw it. That's why Australians have a saying we would do well to remember: "Never sharpen a boomerang!"

When we help others we ultimately help ourselves. When we hurt others, we hurt ourselves, too. The "least of these" brings out the best in us, and gives assurance that an unadvertised kindness has no shelf life.

So the next time we have a chance to care for someone seemingly unimportant – to help a customer who is brusque, to visit an elderly person in a nursing home, to take a pie to the new neighbor, to assist the employee whose wife is undergoing chemotherapy – remember these magical words of the original Extra-Miler. For when we serve the least of these we do the most. Who knows how far the quiet ripples caused by our casually thrown pebbles of kindness will go? Perhaps they will lap the globe and come back full circle to our own shores bringing with them a tidal wave of blessing.

I believe the "10" on Bob Love's retired jersey that hangs high at the United Center in Chicago is a score, not merely a number. "Tens" are Extra-Milers, often in disguise, though a story about kindness can rarely be suppressed forever. If you don't believe me, ask Marco to tell you about an unassuming guy named Bob. Extra-Milers care about others, which means that we should, too.

Now let's do it.

Chapter 9: Extra-Milers Change Those with Whom They Walk

"I tell you the truth, unless you change and become
like little children, you will never enter the kingdom
of heaven."
~ Jesus

Secret #9

Effective leaders have the ability to bring about desirable change through the proper use of influence. Enter a boardroom full of people with impressive titles. It is not always the CEO or president who truly leads the group. The one who can bring about change through influence trumps all comers. You can bank on it.

So, behold a child, an unlikely but highly effective leader. My wife and I have four children and six grandchildren. I sometimes wonder who has influenced whom most over the years; the first, second, or third generation? In my opinion the decision might come down to a photo finish.

And did I mention the animals? Although Caligula is said to have appointed his horse to be a Roman senator, in the main all creatures great and small have rarely held executive titles. Yet, who can dispute the power of animals to influence human behavior?

For example, animal owners will drive through a blizzard to pick up just the right chow for their pet. Nearly extinct tiny fish have halted the building of major dams. Endangered nesting birds have stopped multinational companies from felling forests. Dogs and cats regularly wrap their owners around their hearts so tightly that they'll forgo a major purchase or a family vacation so that Fluffy can have a life-saving operation.

Leadership isn't about being a red-faced, desk-pounding, I-want-it-now business ogre. The prophet Isaiah spoke of the day when, "The wolf will lie down with the lamb, the leopard will lie down with the goat, the calf and the lion and the yearling together; and a little child will lead them." The smallest and least of God's creatures has a disproportionate power to influence and, thereby, to lead.

When I was in graduate school our eldest daughter, Tammy, who was then three, invented a couple of imaginary friends. While the capacity to see the invisible is usually the domain of mystics or the insane, in a young child it is frequently normative, or at least I was so informed by more seasoned parents from whom my wife and I sought advice at the time.

It was not lack of attention or the absence of companionship that motivated Tammy's flights of fancy. In retrospect I suppose she was secretly longing to have brothers and sisters, like many of her peers. In any case, two "children" of unknown age and origin, covert to everyone except our daughter, moved in with us.

I remember vividly when the pair surreptitiously became part of our little family. It was at the beginning of the Christmas season. Tammy, my wife and I were grocery shopping. After loading our purchases into the car we began to pull out of the lot. Suddenly Tammy whimpered, "We're leaving Bee-Bee and Boo-Boo in the store!"

My perplexed look told my wife that I had not yet been notified of our newly extended parental responsibilities. (In fact, she had made the discovery only a little earlier in the day.) With a sigh, then a muffled laugh, she briefed me on this latest development. I was told that Bee-Bee and Boo-Boo were the names of Tammy's imaginary friends. At that moment in her mind the intrepid pair was back in the grocery store, possibly wandering through the seasonal eggnog display in the dairy section.

Feeling quite sheepish, I returned with Tammy to the store in search of the invisible kids, offspring of my imaginative daughter. We found them, sure enough. On return to the car I went through the motions of opening the door, even role-playing helping her new companions into the back seat. She animatedly moved over for them. All seemed well, at least for that evening.

The episode was both humorous and upsetting. My research over the next few days revealed that this stage of her young life would probably soon pass, like so many other childish things do. And it would have passed, too, except that my patience became frayed before Tammy was prepared to give up on Bee-Bee and Boo-Boo. In my mind something had to be done, and sooner rather than later.

Throughout the weeks of Advent the imaginary siblings with outlandish names accompanied us everywhere. They got involved in all sorts of family activities, which I didn't recall them being invited to join.

Then one day while passing a pet store with an attractive Christmas display I was gripped by an idea. It seemed to be a stroke of genius from the heavens! Why not personify Bee-Bee and Boo-Boo via a couple of small animals? I could explain to Tammy that, while her imaginary friends weren't visible, she could make them so. Her friends would morph into small animals.

Hence, on Christmas Eve we made an elaborate pilgrimage to the pet store. Bee-Bee and Boo-Boo materialized before Tamara's eyes in the form of a pair of golden hamsters. They were quite inexpensive, costing only 97¢ each. We bought a cage, some cedar chips, a little food, and voila, Tammy was fully rehabilitated! Her playmates had suddenly become real. Perhaps I, at long last would get some of that Christmas peace that had eluded me since the arrival of Bee-Bee and Boo-Boo.

From that moment on Bee-Bee and Boo-Boo were no longer the invisible twins. She thoroughly liked her new fuzzy pals, who in her mind alternated between being intimate companions and tiny siblings. However, we soon found that we had exchanged an imaginary problem for an all-too real one.

Bee-Bee and Boo-Boo turned out to be a couple of bonafide characters. Like many of their species they were hyperactive, full of energy, and capable of spending most of the night scurrying about their cage in a blaze of unabated activity. More than once I was forced to get up in the wee hours of the morning to oil their miniature Ferris wheel, which they used unremittingly. In our cramped apartment all sounds were amplified. The hamsters' nightly forays were not exactly an inducement to sound sleep.

To make matters worse the hamsters were natural escape artists, virtual Houdini's of the animal world. They seemed to yearn for unknown adventure beyond the bars of their neat wire house. When not engaged in sleeping, hiding food, or organizing their shoebox home, they were invariably occupied with trying to break out of confinement. At first periodically, and then more frequently, they succeeded.

In spite of their flair for gaining freedom, however, they were rather predictable in terms of their hideout once their release from incarceration was achieved. Our apartment sofa had hollow arms and they would predictably head for its comfort and security, like a couple of banditos riding for the border after a holdup. When I discovered that they had fled, I would put my head next to the divan and could count on the sound of their rummaging about within the bowels of their furniture-fortress.

But knowing where they were and getting them to come out and surrender were different matters entirely. After enticing them with generous bribes of corn and seeds I could usually get them back into their cage, but not without extreme difficulty. One false move would send them racing back into their dark cavern and the entire process would start anew, with Bee-Bee and Boo-Boo now far less inclined to let their sniffing noses be seen a second time.

Of course, Tammy loved all this commotion. The new friends entertained her continuously and I, for my part, unwittingly added to the show. Little did I know then how comical my antics must have appeared to her, going round after round with tiny hamsters a fraction of my size and usually being bested in the process.

For unknown reasons, Bee-Bee had an abbreviated lifespan, enduring for one more Christmas plus two months. We had a brief burial service for the first half of the infamous twins. Tammy took it all in stride, especially since Boo-Boo was her favorite and he was still scurrying around.

I received my degree from grad school and we proceeded to move to a house in the country. We loved animals of all kinds, so our home soon became a menagerie. In spite of the increased animal population, Boo-Boo kept a high profile and maintained a most favored status. Age did not diminish his wanderlust. His regular breakouts continued throughout his thoroughly unreformed and lengthy hamster life.

Boo-Boo's ultimate end came shortly after his third Christmas. It was only then that I finally realized how a gift given in exasperation to help an imaginative daughter come to grips with reality had become an enduring spiritual lesson for both my wife and me. We had purchased Bee-Bee and Boo-Boo to fill a void in a child's life, but the two of them had gone on to significantly touch two adults as well. For my part I would often come in from arduous hours of study or work, only to find respite by reason of those two 97¢ rascals. The Christmas hamsters, acquired on a whim during the season of joy became a perennial source of pleasure and mirth far exceeding the reach of Advent.

Tammy is now an adult and will only answer to Tamara. She is the mother of two healthy boys and a girl. (Thankfully, none are named either Bee-Bee or Boo-Boo.) Every Christmas we tell the grandchildren about the little creatures who came to live with us one holiday season so long ago. We share with them how the invisible can become real and, that when the real becomes invisible again, as so often it must, it can still exist pleasantly in our memories.

When I hear the first annual Salvation Army bell of the Advent season, I am drawn to memories of Bee-Bee and Boo-Boo. If I happen by the dairy section of the grocery store, and especially when near the eggnog display, I unconsciously think of my daughter's imaginary friends. And I meditate anew about how a little child taught my wife and me to be childlike again, with a couple of interesting tiny actors to flesh out the allegory.

Extra-Milers know that titles and nameplates have little to do with true influence. Two millennia ago a carpenter changed the world. He teaches us still, as he gathers infants and toddlers around him to be part of the lesson we bigger folk are reluctant to learn. Become small to be big, he advises them. Go two miles instead of one, he says to whoever will listen. Speak softly and carry a big stick – a walking stick, that is – a two-mile staff, he suggests.

When I was a little tyke I ran into our house and allegedly left the front door open. I don't remember this bit of dialogue, of course, but our family folklore finds my father barking the dad-like question: "Hey, were you born in a barn?" To which I reputedly replied rather innocently, "Yes, daddy, just like the baby Jesus!"

Most of us weren't born in a barn. But that shouldn't keep us from learning a valuable lesson that comes from the inner recesses of that historical stable. For the "least of these" now teaches us how to lead. At Christmas we are reminded of this anew. Surrounded by bleating sheep and mooing cows, a baby cries.

So let's continue to follow the wobbly footprints of that toddler, leading gradually away from the crèche, ever growing as his parallel steps move steadily toward a hilltop a couple of miles away. Warning: It takes quite a while to traverse that seemingly short distance – 33 years to be exact.

But along the way, from the crib to the cross, from the cradle to the crown, that Extra Mile will change you and me – and everyone else who chooses to make the trek with us.

Chapter 10: Extra-Milers Know Where They Are Headed

"From that time on Jesus began to explain to his disciples that he must go to Jerusalem and suffer many things..."
~ St. Matthew's explanation of Jesus' ultimate purpose

Secret #10

Jesus didn't keep his mission a secret. At an early stage in his ministry he went public with his master plan. He shared with his disciples the who, what, when, why, and where of it all. His intended trajectory would lead straight through the twin townships of pain and suffering. There would be no shortcut to glory. Those who chose to follow him should consider the options. The next proverbial mile wouldn't be a cakewalk, or so he implied.

Of course, some didn't get it. Or they simply refused to believe it. On sunny Galilean days the topics Jesus tended to bring up in casual conversation seemed inane. The bright sunshine served to wash out the ominous clouds of his message. One disciple thought all of the negative talk had gone far enough. Simon Peter, otherwise known as The Mouth, unceremoniously yanked Jesus aside and proceeded to line him up. In his spicy fisherman's brogue he aired his views without concern for who might hear them. In fact, he was loud on purpose. He wanted one and all to know where he stood. C'mon, Master, let's be a little more positive!

Peter: "Lord, what's all this business about beatings and mayhem? Do you have a death wish or something?"

Jesus: "No, Simon, I don't. I love life, as much as you do. So, I'm being upfront in telling you what will happen next. If the script I've been given doesn't suit you, well, then you should make your adjustments now. Forewarned is forearmed."

Peter: "Me, make adjustments? Surely you jest! With all due respect, Jesus, maybe you might want to take that medicine yourself. Let go of the morbidity already. Don't worry; be happy. Lighten up!"

Jesus: "Peter, you may not know it, but that's the enemy talking through you right now. So, I will not listen to another word. As I've said, if you can't or won't follow the road I must take, pick another one. Seek another master. But your blustering and bravado changes nothing. And as for the rest of you (looking at those who'd gathered in response to Peter's raised voice), take up your cross and get in line. Or sign on with a softer rabbi whose message is more to your liking. The choice is yours. I've told you about where my road will lead well ahead of time – in fact, in plenty of time for you to cut and run. So either re-sign – or resign. Dismissed."

Jesus had never given such an in-your-face locker room speech before. So far he had only raised his voice when addressing the scribes and religious leaders. But here he was flushed, clearly not amused, eyes flashing, almost daring any of those gathered nearby to contradict him. With his sandaled feet firmly planted and his hands on his hips, his body language implied that the subject wasn't open for discussion any longer.

None of them would ever forget that moment. An invisible line seemed to have been drawn on the coarse, pebbled beach next to their fishing vessels, the ones they had left to follow him. "Take it or leave it," the line seemed to say. "Cross it and you will probably die with me," it warned.

That night several novice disciples packed their bags. They scurried off, muttering under their breath a protest about "it's his way or the highway", obviously having selected the latter. They preferred the single mile road; the one with no hills or valleys and no surprise turns; the one best defined by boredom and predictability and above all, safety. And by choosing the wide, short road they missed the chance to make history in the company of a man they clearly misunderstood.

It still happens – the misunderstanding that is. Three decades ago I had the chance to start a church in a collar suburb of Chicago. On our new congregation's maiden Sunday I met two men, whom we'll call Bert and Jim. For reasons I've never fully answered to my satisfaction, I asked both men the same initial question: "What would you like to accomplish by the end of your life?"

Bert, who was in his late sixties at the time, said he would be pleased to end his journey with all of his children, grandchildren, and great-grandchildren acknowledging a meaningful spiritual heritage. Jim, at least a decade younger than Bert, replied that he'd like to own a new pick-up truck and live in the Colorado Rockies.

The discrepancy between the values reflected in their responses struck me as odd, even then. One man wished to end his journey with others being blessed. The other fellow wanted the blessing all for himself. Here we had an Extra Mile and a One Mile case study in the making, though I didn't know it at the time.

Years passed. My wife and I were on vacation along the coast of Big Sur in California. The telephone rang. Bert, who had been in a nursing facility for several months, had died. Would I do the funeral when I returned? Why, of course, I'd be honored to do so. I'd be home day after tomorrow. It would be a privilege to preside over the home-going ceremonies for such a dear friend and faithful parishioner.

A couple of hours later as I was packing my bags to go to the airport the phone rang again. Coincidentally, Jim had also died, on the very same day as Bert. Would I do his funeral? I hesitated. My reluctance was born of surprise. I hadn't seen or heard from Jim in a long time. Didn't he have a pastor where he had moved? Wasn't he a member of a parish when he had died? My secretary couldn't give me an answer. So I agreed to do Jim's memorial service the day after Bert's funeral. It was shaping up to be a busy week.

My wife and I flew home. Jetting over the Rockies I thought of the two men I had met 30 years earlier on the very same day. What were the odds of their also dying on the very same day? I wondered if they had met their goals, the ones we had discussed briefly many years before, back when first we met. I would soon find out.

I knew quite a bit about Bert's journey. He had been one of the most committed, sincere spiritual men I had ever known. It wasn't just that he was in his favorite seat (the one to the speaker's left, second row, end of pew) every time the doors were opened. Bert was, well, a very godly man. He didn't say a lot; he walked the talk.

There was almost a patriarchal sheen to Bert. He oozed graciousness. And his family was paramount to him. He constantly entreated me to care for my children because, he would intone in his Finnish accent, "a man's family is his last will and testament". When he would repeat this mantra to me in later years I'd flash back to the first time I met him, and what he'd said about how he wanted to end his sacred journey surrounded by his extended clan.

In contrast to Bert, I'd lost all contact with Jim. He had been part of the congregation's life for a few years, and then he'd suddenly dropped out of everything and moved. I heard that he had divorced his wife and left his family. Rumor had it that he'd gone out west to parts unknown in search of his selfish dream.

Frankly, I was astonished to be the one requested to do Jim's funeral. Before his move we'd had a couple of very direct conversations, during which I had shared with him some matters he clearly was not inclined to hear; issues along the lines of what Bert had often told me, about the importance of building an enduring heritage and investing one's life in family. He had opted to ignore me, so why was I now going to say the last words over him?

The plane landed at O'Hare Airport. My secretary handed me the plans for Bert's funeral. It reflected favorably on his life without any exaggeration. I've done my share of memorials wherein the deceased's laurels had to be burnished undeservedly for the sake of the grieving family. But Bert's service would have more to do with honoring the God he had served consistently for almost nine decades than Jim's. There would be no empty blandishments or exaggerated platitudes associated with Bert's life. (You know what I mean: "He never said a bad word about anyone...") No, Bert was the real deal. His funeral would be an honor for an honorable man.

The church was filled to capacity. People sat close together. The eulogies for Bert were spontaneous and unstoppable. There was plenty of laughter. The tears shed expressed both sorrow and joy. To top it all off, several rows were filled with generations of Bert's descendants, all endued with the same strong spirituality that had made their forbearer such a striking gentleman. Bert had started his journey with the end in mind and he had reached his goal, the Extra Mile marker. Way to go, Bert!

Jim's memorial service was, well, much different to say the least. A mere handful of people was scattered widely through the funeral home, facing an urn holding Jim's ashes. The atmosphere was charged with sadness and regret. Those I knew greeted me civilly enough. But let's just say that there wasn't a huge reservoir of good will in the room.

The story of Jim's demise was whispered in my ear by a couple of emotionally detached relatives. Jim had been insistent on moving to Colorado to fulfill the "dream" he had told me about so long ago. His family refused to go with him, having given in to his wanderlust before only to have his dream turn into their nightmare. He had too often brushed aside their entreaties, in his selfish pursuit of what he insisted would be the crowning achievement of his life.

Leaving family and those who loved him behind, he imagined himself a pioneer on a quest for his new frontier. He ventured to Colorado where he bought a new pick-up truck and built a primitive cabin in the woods, just as he had once said he would. Seeing himself as a modern day Thoreau he lived a Walden-like existence until his death.

His body was neglected, his presence not missed, for nearly a week. Then the postman made the gruesome discovery. I was told that outside his dilapidated Colorado cabin sat his new pick-up truck, still quite shiny except for seven days of accumulated dust. Jim perfunctorily ended his journey on the loneliest of highways, the shortest and most oft traversed, the One Mile road to nowhere.

Let's return to Simon Peter for a moment as he follows Jesus at a distance, trying all the while to decide what to do. He has few options, having left all to follow the Master. How could he face his wife and mother-in-law if he quit being a disciple now? They'd told him to stop chasing these itinerant prophets long ago. He didn't want to hear their I-told-you-so's. He could not bear their reproaches yet again. Therefore, he shut up and tagged along with the band of disciples. However, deep inside he didn't believe what Jesus had said about the path to an early death. The Master would surely wake up to reality, he thought. The cheering crowds near the holy city would change his mind. His increasing popularity and his rise in the political polls would force him to accede to reason. So Peter hiked hopefully with Jesus toward Jerusalem – physically following him close at hand, but emotionally straggling behind.

Palm Sunday seemed to do the trick. The people wanted to make Jesus their king. However, Jesus had returned the donkey, the equivalent of a modern stretch limousine, to its owner when it was all over. The Extra Mile isn't along a paved, easy thoroughfare. I told you, I keep telling you, Peter, that your charted route and mine are not at all the same. Still Simon wouldn't listen. He had another nickname besides Peter (aka The Rock): Hardhead. Peter was known to be as thick as the planks out of which his fishing boat was made. So it was no surprise when Mister Hardhead came up short by one mile. It was that lost mile that would now span the distance between Peter's best dream and his worst nightmare.

Simon Peter, the Rock, the born leader, the know-it-all, had mapped out a wonderful little day trip through Green Pastures, carefully avoiding the Valley of the Shadow of Death. As a result he made one mistake after another during his last week with Jesus. He bragged about his loyalty, but then denied Jesus three times in a row, punctuating his denials with foul curses. He refused to wash feet when servanthood was the order of the day. Suffice it to say, Jesus' final days weren't Peter's best days.

Yet, to his credit, Peter got back on the road again, the Extra Mile road. Even so, legend has it that he almost relapsed toward the end of his life. The story goes that Peter was under the threat of death by the Emperor Nero. He was accused of being a follower of Jesus. Wanting to live to preach another day, he high-tailed it from Rome along the Appian Way.

On the way out of town it is reported that he thought that he spied a familiar face. The person he saw was headed along the Via Appia going in the opposite direction, into Rome. Peter thought that even though the face was partially covered it looked a lot like Jesus. Peter tentatively called out to the shadowy figure that had passed him by. The conversation went something like this...

Peter: "Lord? Jesus? Is that you?"

Traveler: "Yes, Simon, it's me."

Peter: "Jesus, where are you going? Why are you on this road leading into Rome? Don't you know they'll kill you – again? Come with me, Lord. I'm getting out of here while I still can!"

Traveler: "Peter, the larger question is 'quo Vadis?' – where are you going and why are you going there, my old friend?"

Peter: "I'm leaving Rome, Lord. It's not safe anymore. I advise you to come with me. It is better to be a living dog than a dead lion."

Traveler: "Peter, I must go to Rome. I have given you the assignment to suffer for me and, since you apparently won't, I must. Again."

Peter: "Lord, I made that mistake once before. I shall not do so again. I fully accept the road you've chosen for me. I'll return to Rome, if that is your will."

The legendary story of their conversation is admittedly a bit hazy. Maybe it happened; maybe it didn't. But tradition has it that Peter returned to Rome and died, crucified upside down, on the outskirts of that great city. In so doing he finally learned through his death about the Extra Mile; the mile he discounted when younger as unnecessary and vain.

The Extra Mile is the one that Bert planned for and that Jim declined. People who are on the Extra Mile road know where they are headed. It isn't to Colorado and a little cabin and a pick-up truck. It is to a life spent in service for others, our family and friends and even strangers. The outcome is the difference between Jesus and Simon, between Bert and Jim. It is the difference between legacy and tragedy.

It is a choice that starts now.

Let's keep moving...

Chapter 11: Extra-Milers Are Exceedingly Generous

"Give and it will be given to you. A good measure,
pressed down, shaken together and running over,
will be poured into your lap. For with the measure
you use, it will be measured to you."

~ Jesus

Secret # 11

Gratitude and generosity are essential partners when it comes to lasting success. The former is the CEO and the latter is the CFO of our corporate health and happiness. By the same token bitterness and stinginess are uneasy allies, barely able to abide each other. Theirs is a symbiotic relationship. Gratitude and generosity appreciate, whereas bitterness and stinginess depreciate. Wisdom dictates that we join forces with what improves us – and that's where gratitude and generosity come into play.

Jesus said that giving is better than receiving, though he never denied the salutary effects of a well-timed gift or a bonus check. Most people will walk through fire or over glass for a trophy, a medal, or even a kind word. I have received my share of thoughtful gifts and, lest there be any question, the knowledge that someone cares enough to wrap a present or write a note has been a powerful elixir for my sagging spirit on more than one occasion. But when giving and getting are thoughtfully contrasted, giving wins the contest by a remarkable margin.

Why is this so? Because giving is like a Roth IRA, and getting is more akin to a conventional IRA. A Roth IRA requires the investor to pay taxes up front (that's the downside), but the withdrawals are made tax-free (which is the upside). A regular IRA lets you invest capital initially without much ado, but then taxes are taken from the ultimate disbursements forever. "See me now or see me later," says the taxman, "but you shall most certainly see me."

What has this to do with generosity or the lack of it? Well, one-mile people are usually "getters". They don't want to pay "taxes" on investments now (or ever for that matter). They are inclined to believe they need to only make contributions to their favorite charity, which usually tends to be themselves.

Extra-Milers, by contrast, are proactively generous. They are not only prone to lavishly share their treasure, but their time and talent are made available as well. Indeed, if we aren't careful the giving of our money can become a mere placebo for sharing a listening ear or lending a helping hand. Sharing our money is a good thing, but not everything.

One of the most thoughtful Extra Mile gifts I ever received was from an older friend named Max, who was far enough ahead of me on the path of life to have been my father. When my own dad died unexpectedly, Max was in the middle of a high-level corporate meeting. Though he shared responsibility for nearly ten thousand employees, Max left what he was doing and made the trip to be by my side. His visit lasted only a few minutes, but I have never forgotten his thoughtfulness. It was what I needed at that moment. I needed his presence more than his presents. I didn't realize it until later, but what he did in giving me his time was more valuable than money or flowers or a card.

But Max was that way with everyone. Years later, when Max retired, we literally traveled around the globe together. He jotted down the names of the people he met, always on the back of a number 10 envelope, which usually stuck out of his shirt pocket at an angle along with his engineer's pencil. Long after I'd forgotten certain individuals we had met, Max would bring their names up in casual conversation. ("Remember Thomas, the man we had supper with in Bangalore?" Or, "Did you ever learn John's wife's name, the fellow who gave us the jitney ride that night in Manila?") Too often I had forgotten the event and the person, but Max seldom did.

It was part of his continuous full service treatment. No wonder he excelled in business, in his neighborhood, as a family man, at church, and as a friend. Though Max was one of the most generous gentlemen I have known, he rarely gave lavish gifts to individuals. When he would take me out to eat, it was always to one of those steak houses where you order by number while standing in line. Though at work he could call for the company plane or a corporate limo at a moment's notice, away from the executive suite he preferred flannel shirts and a simple lifestyle. He would introduce himself to those he met as "an engineer", humbly neglecting to mention his many patents and his impressive job title of "Chief Engineer" of a multinational locomotive concern.

Before his passing, Max's wife, Audrey, had a stroke that left her in need of constant assistance. Max and Audrey were both generous. However, it fell to Max to care for his spouse. Let's just say that, for all his thoughtfulness, I'd never visualized Max as an attentive caregiver. He was used to giving orders, not taking them. Yet, when push came to shove, he was equal to the task. While his resources allowed him to provide Audrey with the best professional help, in his mind that never would replace the aid that only he, a loving husband, could provide.

When Max died he left the bulk of his estate to a college, a church, a drug treatment center, and several philanthropic organizations. He had been frugal for a good purpose: Others. On his desk were some of his famous number ten envelopes, with many names written out in his neat engineer's block print. And as I gave the sermon at his funeral, I thought back to the morning when a busy industry boss took the time to visit a bereaved friend in need of a tight hug and a quick prayer. Generosity pays dividends, even postmortem.

Jesus' proverb about generosity found at the beginning of this chapter begs that we pause and mull it over. Like all aphorisms, it is a principle, not a law. Sadly, there are some very giving people who rarely receive reciprocally, not to speak of bountifully, in this life. There are many parents in nursing homes that once gave lavishly, perhaps too much so, to their children who now visit them only when in need of another "loan". And some of the most generous people I know have become tagged as givers, to the point of being excluded from receiving needed help when in dire straits themselves.

But the proverb still stands as a reliable generalization: "Give – and it will be given to you". Jesus was referring to the practice of using one's garment to carry grain home following a trip to the local mill. Stingy farmers might find that they took home less than they had brought in to be ground up by the primitive millstones. (The undetected "deduction" was probably made to "settle" past discrepancies between Farmer Scrooge and the mill owners.) On the other hand, kind farmers could count on fair treatment, in the form of taking home exactly what they had carried to the mill, though no more and no less.

And then there were the generous harvesters. In the past they had been kind or helpful to the ones operating the heavy grinding equipment. Maybe they had heard about a family in need and had sent over a few extra bushels of wheat as benevolence. How could the appreciative mill worker ever say thanks, he had wondered at the time? Now he knew, for it was payback time. The unsuspecting unselfish farmer was told to extend his garment as far as it would go. Scoop after scoop of ground grain was shoveled into his apron, until the quantity clearly exceeded what he had brought with him to the mill.

Imagine the quizzical look on the recipient's face. How had this happened? Surely a mistake had been made. He had been given way too much. "No," he was assured by the mill owner, "you got no more than what you gave. Your imagination must be working overtime. Again."

Sound familiar? Extra-Milers are not strangers to this type of phenomenon. Generosity is initially quietly offered to a person in need. Then, years later, the covert investment of a few dollars given or a few minutes shared returns in spades. What's happening here? How did this occur? You paid the "taxes" up front and now you're receiving unexpected dividends – much more and much later.

But behold the one who lives selfishly, never venturing beyond that first required mile or, even worse, not even walking the full single mile required by the ancient law. You know the kind of person I'm describing. It's the clock-watcher at work; the class-cutting student in college; the "it's not my job" salesperson at the store. They are part of a fraternity of millions named Iota Delta Kappa ("I Don't Care"). The initiation rites include successfully keeping to yourself what rightfully belongs to you, never sharing. The group's motto is: "What's mine is mine and what's yours will be mine, too – if I have any say in the matter."

A number of Chinese graduate students attended our church several years ago. They had come to America to earn advanced degrees, and then planned to return to their home country upon graduation. We invited them to attend the services, for both cultural and spiritual reasons.

The first couple of months they were full of questions. After they had surveyed our buildings and grounds one of their perennial questions was, "Who pays for all of this?" They were invariably surprised to find that the parishioners did so and, furthermore did so voluntarily, even joyfully. Over time I crafted a staple answer to their questions about why our members were so generous. I would tell them: "Capitalism says: What is mine is mine, so I can keep it. Communism says: What is yours is mine, so you must share it. But Christianity says: What is mine may be all mine, but I want to share it with you." The urge to give is not generated by law; it is motivated by grace.

The Chinese students tended to understand this formula. It is, after all, a universal principle as true in America as in China. "Give and it will be given unto you." Go the Extra Mile. Be exceedingly generous, not so that you can receive in return, but because it is right and fulfilling. Indeed, the one who is fulfilled is often filled-full before life's end, or so the inspired proverb suggests.

King Solomon was wise and open-handed. He commented in the Book of Proverbs: "One man gives freely, yet gains even more; another withholds unduly, but comes to poverty."

Generosity has a tipping point. There is a fine line between saving and stinginess. If one's life has no wiggle room for sharing the bounty and if the secret slush fund is for private use only, ruin is certainly around the corner.

My mother was always a model of generosity. Whatever I've gleaned on the subject was learned while following her around the harvest field that is called "Life". In our kitchen, while I was growing up, Mom had a crocheted saying prominently displayed on a wall. It read: "Love ever gives, forgives, outlives. It ever stands with open hands. And while it lives, it gives. For this is love's prerogative – to give and give and give."

When your defining characteristic is stinginess, your gross intake may be more than the generous person today, but the net "bottom line" will inevitably come up short tomorrow. This is equally true in business, relationships, spirituality, civics, marriage – you name it. The maxim may be counterintuitive, but it works. The more you give, the more you get. It is a tried and true maxim: God and nature will always give more through you than to you. If you are a conduit rather than a safety deposit box, life will surprise you by giving you far more than you need. Why? Providence gives to those who will pass it on. God shares with those he knows will share in turn.

In Israel there are two major bodies of water, the Sea of Galilee and the Dead Sea, joined by the serpentine Jordan River. The Sea of Galilee is teeming with fish. The Dead Sea has no aquatic life at all, hence its name. Why?

Look at a map. The Sea of Galilee (which is actually a lake) both receives and gives out fresh water. The melted snows of Mount Hermon to the north feed it with an unending supply of pristine water, while the Jordan River to the south becomes an equally generous outlet. As a result the in-take and out-take makes the famous northern lake a constant freshwater funnel, channeling its abundance to those who live to the south. Getting gives way to giving, and the net result is that the Sea of Galilee overflows with life.

However, the Dead Sea to the south merely takes in, reluctantly "giving" its supply away only by forced evaporation.

Indeed, the Jordan River expectantly flows in to the Dead Sea, but absolutely nothing flows out. The result is a giant and ever-shrinking oversized saline puddle, with no life of its own. At the northern shore, where the River Jordan disgorges its flow, the Dead Sea gladly accepts its donations with open hands. But no sooner does the Dead Sea receive the entry of the river's moist bounty than its open hands become tightly clenched, miserly fists. The Dead Sea is a parable, whispering to us that Scrooges usually end up badly.

There's an age-old lesson here: When people stop giving, by definition, they start dying. Sadly, some folks die early and are buried late. We mistake this for longevity. The truth is that many tightwads have as their epitaph something like: "Died at 35; buried at 83." Cheapness kills us prematurely. We are interred long after our expiration date is up. Such people are seldom remembered, except to be vilified. There are no lasting memorials for cheapskates.

On the other hand, there is no expiration date stamped on our generosity.

Yet, may we take cheer in the reality that there's always the chance for a resurrection of sorts, a second chance, an epiphany before all hope is lost. So, all would-be pilgrims on this Extra Mile journey, like Lazarus of old, let us rise from the dark tomb of penury and emerge into the daylight of generosity's better way. It works. I say it again: It works! It will make a difference in our homes, in commerce, and in society. And, what's more, going the Extra Mile all the way to generosity is an enjoyable and fruitful trek. Let's continue to hike onward and upward.

MILE 2

Chapter 12: Extra-Milers Enjoy Life and Laughter

"Blessed are you who weep now, for you will laugh."
~ Jesus

Secret # 12

Humor is a funny thing. A real thigh-slapper for one person is a groaner to another. Different countries and cultures express humor uniquely. A joke in Asia cannot be readily translated into English. Men and women worldwide have alternative perceptions of what constitutes a ready wit.

Recently my wife and I were at a gathering with three other married couples. One of the men told a good, clean joke. Upon hearing the punch line, all of the guys doubled over in a simultaneous fit of mirth. The wives, on the other hand, just looked at one another quizzically for a few seconds. Then one of the ladies muttered "Sick!" The other three ladies, like a perfectly harmonized chorus, intoned solemn agreement. No wonder men and women often have what is best described by the prison warden in the movie Cool Hand Luke as "a failure to communicate."

Humor can be analyzed and scrutinized. But, like an orchid, too much handling ruins it. I have concluded that an adaptation of Supreme Court Justice Potter Stewart's definition of pornography may apply to various forms of humor: "I know it when I see [or hear] it."

Humor is most certainly is a personal thing, but must be sufficiently communal to cause a group of similarly minded people to laugh with other people. (That's why laugh tracks are often added to pre-taped comedy shows on television.)

All of us want to participate. Let others tell you of the release of endorphins or write articles about the psychology of humor, but what I know is that I feel good after a sidesplitting laugh, as though my nerves have taken a mini-vacation. No wonder comedians make so much money. Paying big bucks for a show every now and then is cheaper than the never-ending cost of medication for chronic colitis or frayed nerves.

But what has laughter to do with Jesus? And what has good humor to do with those who accompany him along the Extra Mile? Does a dour Roman soldier require a jester to carry his bags? Is comedic expression part of our extra-mile portfolio? Must we build a repertoire of jokes and gags to entertain those we are called to serve, whose heavy bags we have been shanghaied to carry?

Few Hollywood interpretations of Jesus' life find him smiling on more than a few frames of celluloid. When he does try to show any kind of joviality the expression can best be described as pinched; a pained, reluctant attempt at joy. Film directors invariably do their best to turn Jesus into a sourpuss.

We've grown up with the perception that the Almighty must be in a perpetual bad mood, authenticated by tragic world events and gloomy economic indicators, which a more jovial deity would most certainly not tolerate. He looms at the edge of the swimming pool, like an irritated cosmic lifeguard, longing to have an excuse to blow his celestial whistle and shout, "Everybody out, right now! You're having way too much fun."

Would it surprise us that Jesus actually had a good sense of humor? His listeners probably guffawed at more than one of his dry comments or allegories, which tend to lose some of their original punch when translated into our western language and culture. When Jesus spoke of a camel going through the eye of a needle, or of a man with a log in his own eye trying to remove a splinter from his neighbor's eye, his audience probably roared with raucous laughter.

So why are we not equally tickled? Perhaps it is because the most difficult thing to do cross-culturally is to translate humor into another language accurately. The ultimate test to demonstrate one's grasp of a new dialect is found in the natural expression of humor via the newly learned language. If you are telling a joke to intercultural friends and you get a heart-felt laugh in return, congratulations! You now know their folklore and the subtleties of their language. When you connect cross-culturally through humor, and your audience doesn't laugh at you but with you, you've graduated to a higher level of interaction. Humor is a cultural bridge of sorts.

All of the Extra-Milers I know and esteem have a well-developed sense of humor. Without it, survival along the tortuous two-mile road is difficult. Jesus knew the power of laughter. And so must his disciples, both ancient and modern. We bend or we break. Humor keeps us elastic, less inclined to take life too seriously.

A scowling centurion, beckoning a man to carry his load, has lessened negative influence over that person if the one singled out has chosen an amusing interpretation to the situation. One's body and time may be unwillingly coerced, but it doesn't follow that we must give the soldier our souls.

We all do a better job when we can laugh with, not snap at, already exasperated customers. We excel to the extent that we can turn fury into funny. This emotional alchemy, whereby we can make sweet lemonade from sour lemons, allows our tightly wound tension to be transformed into gentle teasing. In so doing we can defuse a potentially explosive moment.

This principle brings to mind a now famous event that originated in August of 1964. The editor of a major magazine was forced to fly home unexpectedly from an overseas trip. He was suffering from a recurrent fever and constant unexplainable pain, especially in his joints.

Within days of returning stateside the editor couldn't get out of bed. Extensive tests revealed that he had a rare disease that attacks the fibrous substance holding the human cells together. In other words, his body's "cement" was not doing its job. In a very real sense he was coming unglued.

Ugly nodules appeared beneath his skin. A panel of doctors, after looking over the medical reports, judged the man's chance of recovery to be only one in five hundred. To make matters worse, he was caught in a medical Catch 22. While he desperately needed to get his endocrine system working properly again, the disease caused his body to reject the very drugs that were intended to help him.

So, since he had nothing to lose, he decided to try a new and untested course of action. With his doctor's approval, he began taking massive doses of vitamin C. But along with the large amounts of vitamin C he also self-prescribed copious amounts of daily laughter. The fire of his self-induced merriment was ignited mainly by humorous movies and funny stories. He soon made a rather amazing discovery: Ten minutes of belly-laughter had an anesthetic effect that afforded him two hours of pain-free sleep. Instead of his body falling apart, he was getting himself together again.

Over a period of time he literally laughed himself back to health. He then proceeded to write a book about his unique experience, which ended up on The New York Times bestseller list for 40 weeks. The book was called The Anatomy of an Illness. The author's name: Norman Cousins. In the book, Cousins makes reference to verses about laughter in the Bible, then remarks: "I was greatly elated to discover that there is a physiological basis for the ancient theory that laughter is good medicine."

Jesus said that we may first cry, but eventually we will laugh – just like Norman Cousins. Why this strange and wonderful process? It is because tears usually come to us in the first mile of any endeavor. It is at the start of a job, a marriage, or an exploit that we encounter pain and suffering. Ask anyone who has taken up exercise after a year as a couch potato or who returns to college in their forties. Pain precedes progress. Sandal blisters cause the uninitiated short-distance hiker to recoil from the thought of going beyond the single mile marker. There is little joy in the first mile of any journey. So, how can there possibly be anything except more pain when walking two miles?

But the Extra Mile is amazingly much happier than the first. The benefits of the Extra Mile show up on the horizon of life eventually, yet never before the first mile has been completed. And rarely is the additional mile welcomed by the man or woman who is disinclined to allow for a theology of joy, exhibited best by life-preserving peals of laughter in the midst of stress. The iconic "smiley face" sticker is less a childish yellow reward for a job well done, and more a sign of achievement as we walk the path toward a blessed tomorrow.

Abraham Lincoln, who was stressed constantly by the rigors of the Civil War, maintained that without humor he could never have prevailed. Witnesses reported that his laugh was like the neighing of a horse. He would regularly call passers-by into his office to share his latest tall-tale, invariably followed by loud laughter. To a large lady, who sat on his hat, he said: "Madam, I could have told you it wouldn't fit if you had merely asked me first." His retorts and wit allowed him to bear the heavy burdens of the Civil War in much the same way as you and I can carry our centurion's knapsack.

John Kennedy also had an excellent sense of humor. He was a master at deflecting tough press conference questions with a witty turn of a phrase. Camelot was more of an attitude than a reality. In the throes of the Cold War he still made time to smile. JFK showed us how to respond to stress with a healthy sense of humor.

Ronald Reagan, immediately after John Hinckley shot him, said to his worried wife: "Honey, I forgot to duck!" And to the doctors who were about to remove the life-threatening bullet, he commented: "I hope you are all Republicans." Reagan, well into his seventies, probably won reelection the moment he said to Walter Mondale during a crucial televised debate: "I will not make age an issue in this election. I will not exploit the youth and inexperience of my opponent for personal gain!"

However, in the past leaders and potentates had trouble keeping their humor quotient high. For this reason court jesters frequently accompanied kings of yore regularly. Those ancient mirth-makers in their silly outfits were often the monarch's most trusted confidants, having the rank of a presidential cabinet member today. The jester's assignment was a serious one: to help the ruler regain perspective by laughing his troubles away.

Indeed, a laugh is sorely needed if we are to serve others effectively. This holds true in arenas other than politics or business. Lee Tuttle, in Profiles of the 20th Century Giants, says all 24 great Christian leaders about whom he writes had the gift of humor – the only characteristic they shared in common. Why, then, have Christians and religious people gained a reputation for being so somber, dour, and scowling?

In Early Church history the clergy of the Greek Orthodox churches came together to tell humorous stories the day after Easter. They concluded that it was a joyous occasion and hilarity was needed, especially on "the day after" such an important event.

In William Shakespeare's The Taming of the Shrew, a servant says: "Frame your mind to mirth and merriment, which bars a thousand harms and lengthens life." With the current emphasis on nutrition it has been discovered that what is "eating us" is more frequently the real problem rather than what we are eating. Wellness is not just the absence of illness. Our minds and emotions speak to our bodies, and the interaction is not always pleasant. Humor helps to make the conversation between body, soul, and spirit more harmonic.

If we made children the CEOs, the salespeople, and the leaders of our organizations we would probably be better off. The average four year old laughs once every four minutes, whereas the average adult laughs merely fifteen times per day (and only three of those giggles turn into belly laughs). Small wonder that Jesus suggested to his disciples that they needed to become like little children to follow him more effectively.

What happens to us on the way to so-called maturity? Somehow we confuse childishness (which should be admittedly cast off) with childlikeness (which should be more fully cultivated). Laughter, good humor, the twinkle-in-the-eye look of mischief given to us at infancy – these should be in the hip pocket of all would-be Extra-Milers of every age.

When I was in my mid-twenties I helped negotiate the purchase of a television station. The seller was a well-known business tycoon, powerful, respected, and even feared. His limo idled to take him wherever his business might call him. But when it was time for lunch he always stayed behind to dine alone. We were told that he had ulcers, that he usually had crackers and milk for lunch. I came to notice that he never laughed. He was a good enough man, I suppose, but not a true Extra-Miler. Life had weighed him down, flattening out his smile into a scowl.

Jesus said that joy is an important trait for all Extra-Milers on the double-duty trail we have been called to share. It matters little, I suppose, to the one who has no intention of going more than one mile. However, if there is a cross and an eventual resurrection in one's future, it would be good to keep his adage in mind: Weep now, laugh later. And laugh we will, one day, with a hilarity that will resonate deeply and make our previous sorrow a faint memory.

So let's keep walking and laughing, laughing and walking, for it's a big part of our Extra Mile credo.

MILE 2

Chapter 13: Extra-Milers Go Over and Beyond the Call of Duty

"For I tell you that unless your righteousness
surpasses that of the Pharisees and the teachers of the
law you will certainly not enter the kingdom of
heaven."
~ Jesus

Secret # 13

The Congressional Medal of Honor is not bestowed upon West Point cadets when they graduate. Nor is it dispensed to soldiers preparing for their first battle. The highest military medal is not handed out for merely doing one's duty. A soldier must do something more than graduate from an academy or march in step with others to qualify for the nation's most coveted award.

Even injury in battle isn't enough. The men and women who suffer harm in combat should certainly be decorated with some distinguishing insignia, but the Medal of Honor is rightly reserved for the very few. The Purple Heart and the Medal of Honor are quite different in status and purpose.

The Medal of Honor is such a high commendation that President Harry Truman once remarked that he would rather have courageously earned the right to wear the distinguishing blue-ribbon-and-star insignia around his neck than to be the President. Only 3,512 of the medals have been awarded since its establishment in 1862. Since the start of World War II, more than 50 percent of the medals have been presented posthumously. It is clearly not a pendant you can buy at a flea market.

The stipulations for the medal are exacting. The potential recipient must have behaved with such gallantry on the battlefield, that his or her life was placed in serious jeopardy on behalf of others. "Over and beyond the call of duty" is the noble citation's motto. It is no wonder then, that half of the recipients are in the grave when their valor is recognized, when they are finally thanked by a grateful nation.

Our country's appreciation for patriotism comes in the form of a five-pointed star inscribed with a single word: "Valor". Is it worth the sacrifice? We cannot poll those who paid the ultimate price. However, the living recipients universally respond with affirmation.

Most of the Medal of Honor winners indicate they had never viewed themselves as heroes, as particularly brave, prior to the manifest exploit for which they received the hallowed award. Indeed, most say that even after the passage of time they still don't feel particularly worthy to be singled out for the adulation.

Most shun the national spotlight that was unexpectedly turned on them following their heroic effort.

So, how do we explain that nineteen of the soldiers who won this medal then went on to win a second one in an encore act of super-valor? Were these repeated heroic deeds mere coincidences? I think not. There are rather ordinary people lurking among us whose Extra Mile dedication quietly prepares them for a sudden encounter with history, causing both peers and superiors to salute in amazement.

It is my theory that every great action is the result of many smaller actions. This is as true on the negative scale as for the positive. For example, a person involved in a serious traffic accident doesn't suddenly decide to hit-and-run. Certainly the accused driver may later blame panic or momentary loss of reason for the lapse in judgment that mitigated his or her eventual arrest. But my bias is that careful examination will likely turn up a string of smaller evasive decisions. Most often there is an earlier pattern of running from responsibility, one that goes undetected until a major crisis uncovers the perpetrator's character flaw.

Few people become heroes or villains by way of a single isolated incident. Our base or noble thoughts trigger our deeds. Both inner cowardice and hidden bravery surface given sufficient time. When added together our smallest actions ultimately lead to great success or tragic failure. Then one day we either find ourselves inexplicably running from responsibility or into a firefight as if by instinct. How does that happen? I submit that it is instinct, inbred via a thousand smaller decisions that we have made since childhood. In the military what follows is a private court-martial for dereliction of duty or a very public trip to the White House to be given the Medal of Honor by the President of the United States.

The ancient Pharisees and teachers of the law, to whom Jesus made ready reference, aspired to look good. They wanted to be given medals, but without any effort or sacrifice. They were more concerned with style than substance. In military parlance their interest was about the braid on their shoulders, the "fruit salad" on the uniform, the omnipresent shiny medals – rather than in actual achievement. They were good at the talk rather than the walk. As they say in Texas, "They were all hat and no cattle."

Their spin-doctoring and carefully cultivated image managing never quite made up for the deficiencies between what was so and what appeared to be so. They were politicians, not statesmen; hucksters, not true ministers; cowards, not heroes. They were masters of first-mile living. If you saw one of them wearing the dynamic equivalent of a citation for valor, you can be assured that he had bought the faux medal from a roadside vendor. They had never known the smell of gunpowder or the heat of battle.

At the appointed times of daily prayer the Pharisees would deliberately move toward the temple or synagogue, ever a little on the tardy side. It was their plan to be fashionably late. The accepted rule of etiquette was that when the hour struck for prayer you were to stop perfunctorily, wherever you were at that very instant. If you were in the middle of a busy road then right there you started chanting, swaying, and praying. Everyone would then see you doing your sacred duty and marvel at your piety. Who would know that you didn't really care one whit about actual prayer? It was in the seeming to be, not the actual being, that the legend was created.

And did I mention the trumpets? Yes, the trumpets were part of the mystique as well. When the Pharisees and scribes were giving alms multiple horn tooters, kind of like a New Orleans-style Dixieland band, accompanied them as they journeyed to the offering baskets. The musical message had little to do with getting the attention of the poor. It was all about inviting the attention of the crowds. Giving, like prayer, was an exercise in pretense.

On fasting days the same teachers of the law would go to the open market. Their lofty religious status guaranteed that they'd be offered free food, like first century godfathers picking out the best oranges at a fruit stand, knowing all the while that there would be no charge. But, no, they couldn't eat – not today, anyway. Their deliberately drawn, sad faces had the desired effect on the crowds. Even though they had probably only gone without food for a few hours they appeared to be emaciated. Thus they reveled in undeserved adulation.

Indeed, the conventional thinking was that these were revered sanctified men, prepared to risk death in their pursuit of holiness. They would not accept the succulent fruit, extended toward them by admiring merchants, not even free. Everyone looked at them and thought, as was intended: "What valiant fellows these are, going without food for the sake of God. They shun the very morsel that made Adam fall. They should be highly decorated."

Jesus, by contrast, was always ready to exceed true expectations, both when his life was in jeopardy and on ordinary occasions. He was never one to toot his own horn, though his disciples were occasionally inclined to give in to the celebrity moment. However, when the disciples reflected much later on the life and ministry of their master, they summarized his life thus: "...he went about doing good and healing *all* [italics mine] who were under the power of the devil..." (Acts 10:38).

There is a sense of fullness, of completion, in that little word "all". No one was sent away unfulfilled. No one was left behind. Everyone had his or her needs met. Duty could have been easily limited to the first 50 infirm people to limp in. That would certainly be enough for one day's work, even for Rabbi Jesus. But Jesus wanted to go beyond the minimum; his call was to exceed sterile duty. He had the same can-do attitude every morning when he got up and every night when he went to bed. I propose that he even may have dreamed about it during his sleeping hours. Jesus was a 24/7-servant leader. There was nothing haphazard about his perennial availability or his unflagging sense of responsibility.

Of course, Jesus did what he did because he was propelled by a strong sense of divine mission. He was gripped by it. His grand purpose in life was not to punch a clock. He knew he had been sent to this planet for a purpose and that no one else could do what he had been uniquely shaped to perform. It was this sense of mission that caused him to rise each day, go to bed each night.

Western culture strives to convey the illusion that all that glitters is actually gold. We idolize flimsy celebrities rather than emulating legitimate heroes. The two-dimensional life-size cutouts of movie stars and singers that are displayed at media stores are not unlike the Pharisees of yore. They were and are lightweights, like the chaff driven away by the wind, just in different millennia. Don't expect any of them to be in the short line that leads to the bestowment of the Medal of Honor, in whatever field of endeavor.

Extra-Milers aren't interested in merely seeming to be. Whether at work, with family, at church, or in the community, the objective is always the same: Over and beyond the call of duty. The Mile 2 lifestyle is for the meek who are not weak. Do the job and the medal may one day be awarded to you. Then again maybe not – at least in this life. Recognition doesn't always come when expected. But it comes.

Responsibility is the greatest ability – greater than preening and seeming to be. It is at the Extra Mile marker that the medals are distributed, many if not most posthumously. And it is there that the façade of the Pharisee is shown for what it is. Good people do end up in first place, but usually after they've sweated the Extra Mile.

Let's keep moving toward that higher destiny. Let's go over and beyond. It's worth the Extra Mile.

MILE 2

Chapter 14: Extra-Milers Let Bygones Be Bygones

"Forgive and you will be forgiven."
~ Jesus

Secret # 14

On my office desk sits a tiny faded black-and-white photo of a dwarf and a giant. I knew them both, back when I lived as a child in the Dominican Republic. And though they have long since "slipped the surly bonds of earth", the dynamic duo still speaks to me each day in that yellowing, 50-year old snapshot.

Lape is the little one. He wouldn't have won an argument with a yardstick. He had a full-sized head but a tiny, shrunken body. Even so, his lungs were like giant bellows, capable of projecting his piercing voice over great distances. And his large head was home to a great intellect. The picture on my desk shows him grinning mischievously, which is how I best remember him.

Cecilio is the big one, really big. He stands, frozen in time, behind Lape's buggy (actually a homemade wheel chair designed by Lape for his own conveyance). Cecilio appears befuddled, which was his trademark look. The buggy's wheels hide his super-sized feet. His hammy hands seem anxious to push the cart right now; to get moving off the edges of the photograph into the unknown.

Lape and Cecilio were inseparable even though they were at once both opposites and alike in many ways. They both had a radical conversion experience on the same night, in the same church. And both men were called into the ministry almost simultaneously shortly thereafter.

But their call was questioned, if not by them, by many church members. The more logically minded wondered, not without reason, how Lape was going to get around and how Cecilio, with his obvious intellectual limitations, was ever going to preach a sermon worth listening to.

Then God did the remarkable. He made them into a team. He brought the seeming misfits together. That's right, Lape and Cecilio joined forces and together a most unusual, though highly effective, evangelistic team was formed.

Lape designed a buggy for himself and the stuff he carted around and Cecilio built it for him. Lape preached the sermons outdoors with his powerful voice, and then Cecilio would push the cart to the next town. The exercise was repeated hundreds of times. Lape was the brains; Cecilio was the muscle. Their work never flagged because neither cared who got the credit. They needed each other and God needed them together.

I was just a boy when this mighty dwarf-and-giant team was in its heyday. My parents were missionaries. I remember little

Lape and giant Cecilio coming to our home quite often, always unannounced, except for the sound of the cart's wheels crunching the gravel of our long driveway. They'd come in and we'd all sit under the mango tree in our courtyard, drink rich Dominican coffee, and they would tell stories of what God had done in a recent crusade in some nameless village far off the beaten path.

The missionaries were somewhat awed by the pair, and not without reason. It wasn't unusual for one of them to take a four-wheel drive vehicle into the hinterlands, expecting to blaze a fresh Gospel trail, only to find that Lape and Cecilio had already been there a few months earlier. The strange and wonderful "twins" were the stuff of ministerial legend. They appeared where you expected them least.

But, alas, there came the night that became known as The Great Falling Out. Something occurred of an unhappy nature between the pair. No one ever got the whole story, but the word on the street was that Lape had to use the bathroom at midnight, and Cecilio wasn't of the mind to help him at the moment. Apparently, sleep was more important than service. Whatever it was, it caused a schism between them.

So words were exchanged; heated words, unkind words. Deficiencies were pointed out. ("You have no brains." "Yeah, well you have no brawn.") Yes, it was childish, but dawn found the team tragically dissolved. The words could not be taken back and apparently neither felt inclined to apologize to the other.

"Pero no habia problema," as one might say in that culture. Cecilio was convinced that he could be a good street preacher on his own. But a few days out in a few town squares proved otherwise. He quickly found out that no one would listen to him, and more than a few laughed at his mangled efforts at communication.

Lape thought he could easily find another willing fellow to push him across the island, up hills and down into the valleys. But he soon discovered that there was a dearth of buggy-pushers, especially big strong ones. Lape was soon confined to a dark little house where he sat alone, wishing that his eloquence hadn't been misused to distance his ministry partner.

Fortunately, mutual friends intervened. The dwarf and the giant were eventually reconciled by the very Word they preached. The Dream Team was back together, to everyone's amazement and gratitude.

Lape and Cecilio came to our house more often after that brief lapse. We would spend an hour or two drinking coffee and hearing stories about their ministerial adventures. On those occasions, Lape's contagious laughter and Cecilio's shy giggle affirmed that interpersonal healing among God's people is a necessary miracle.

I look at their photo often. A picture is worth many words. It isn't good to be alone, to serve alone, it whispers to me. I seem to hear them say: "Esteban, remember that we were made for community. You see, mi hijo, Jesus sent his disciples out two-by-two. He still does. Don't ever see your brother (or sister) as a bother. Yes, we did for a while and it was tragic. Even though our separation was for an instant, we suffered great pain and loneliness. We never want to go through that again, nor should you."

Amen, I mumble, amen. You are right, mi hermanos. What one can't do, the other one can. We're all called to be twins in life and ministry, and at times even triplets. Some preach and some push. If we do our part well, God gets all of the glory.

That's what the aging photo of Lape and Cecilio conveys to me. I try to look at it out of the corner of my eye whenever I am interacting with a fellow minister or parishioner, especially one with whom I am out of sorts. It has saved me countless hours of preaching to myself in a lonely room, or pushing an empty buggy down an equally lonely one-mile road for, in a way I am both Lape and Cecilio.

To make a friend may require me to keep one eye closed. To keep a new friend may require me to sometimes keep both eyes closed. Of course, this doesn't mean that I must put up with character flaws or moral lapses in silence. I'm talking about letting folks be themselves within the realm of reason.

We should simultaneously celebrate our diversity and build our unity.

Extra-Milers let negative things go, leave them in God's hands. They know that "we" is more important than "me". Lape and Cecilio in community could synergistically do more than multiplied geniuses and muscle men working alone. So, what God has brought together let us not tear apart. Two are better than one – in just about every realm of relationship.

A bit of Christian doggerel says...

To dwell above with saints we love,

That will be glory.

But to dwell below with saints we know,

That's a different story!

Conflicts are a given in relationships, whether business or family. Let's resolve them quickly and move on. The Extra Mile beckons to all of us. So, let's quit lollygagging around the first milepost, arguing over minutia. Who cares? Allow bygones to be bygones.

So now, pilgrim friends, let's move on even further into the realm of the Extra Mile. Let's join Lape and Cecilio on the road that leads to the success and joy of a meaningful life – that is, if we can just swallow our pride and mend our ways.

Chapter 15: Extra-Milers Learn to Travel with Opposition

"Blessed are those who are persecuted for
righteousness, because theirs is the kingdom of
heaven."
~ Jesus

Secret # 15

Let's face it, most of the events we list under "persecution" are usually misfiled. There's a streak of a martyr's complex within each of us that effectively serves to cover up our personal responsibility in stressful relationships. Therefore, if I declare myself to be "persecuted" it absolves me of guilt and puts the onus of blame on my alleged persecutor.

However, Extra-Milers cannot allow themselves the luxury of the blame game. We should learn to discern when we are genuinely being targeted with undeserved opposition and, alternatively, to accurately recognize when someone is merely expressing honest disagreement. Sometimes people may be opposed to our views because our ideas are truly weak or wrong.

To call the resistance we experience at such times by another name doesn't change reality. We should not try to claim the persecution that entitles us to the kingdom of heaven, promised to Christ's true disciples in the Sermon on the Mount, simply because of differences of opinion. Sorry, but that doesn't qualify as biblical persecution. An argument doesn't equal persecution.

By the same token, there are occasions when we go through tough times that are not of our making. Someone may become a real thorn in the flesh. But such people and seasons, properly managed, can produce a harvest of righteousness in the form of our character being sifted and improved. It is then that the words of Jesus bear the most unexpected and sweetest fruit. Genuine persecution, when accompanied by our ability to respond correctly, leads to heavenly reward not only in the hereafter, but also here and now.

Several decades ago, when I was a youth pastor, I served under a senior pastor who was too critical and, to my way of thinking at the time, often unreasonable. Even in the light of passing years this evaluation is somewhat justified, though not totally. In retrospect the pastor was a good man, but not always a wise one. I learned from him some things that I shouldn't do when leading others. It was often a sort of mentorship by negation.

I made it through the ordeal but throughout the process I almost quit the ministry several times. Almost. I would certainly have given up entirely were it not for Mister Dan, the manager at a store where I worked an additional part time job to pay the bills for myself, my wife, and our newborn daughter.

On one especially bad day I decided to give up the ministry and do something else with my life. It was at a youth-sponsored car wash. The pastor showed up and loudly critiqued the job we were doing to raise money for something not in our meager budget. There were no thanks for our hard work, just carping about the way the cars were being detailed. Even worse, he made his criticisms in front of bystanders in an especially harsh manner.

By that time I had endured my fill of humiliation. So as my wife drove me to my part time job at the store, I drafted a letter of resignation. If this was the ministry I wanted no further part of it!

When I arrived at the store Mister Dan could tell something was amiss. I didn't try to hide my frustration. I told him I was giving up on the ministry. Enough was enough. I had been treated shabbily for the last time. What I wanted to know was if he had a full time position at the store – one that he thought I could fill.

The next thing I knew, Mister Dan was quietly informing his secretary that he and I were going over to the donut shop next door. He told me to order whatever I wanted, paid the tab, and then he calmly asked me to listen to a story he wanted to tell me as I munched on my Krispy Kreme donut and drank my coffee.

It seems that a decade before, when he was a recent college graduate, Mister Dan had been hired as an assistant manager at another store within the chain. The agreement was that he would work on a trial basis for three months, and then would be reviewed to determine his fitness for a full managerial position on a permanent basis. There was an implied promise of steady promotions if things worked out.

Mister Dan told me that at that time, even by his own admission, he was self-assured to the point of cockiness. He smiled when he told me that he came to work the first day in a suit and tie, ready to give orders and set the business world on its ear.

However, his manager was of the old school. The man hadn't graduated from college and had joined the company before a business degree was a requirement. His education had been acquired solely by way of street smarts and practical experience. Indeed he seemed antagonistic toward anyone who was classically educated, and soon it became clear that this prejudice extended in particular to Mister Dan.

So the first day on the job did not go well at all, according to Mister Dan. The manager introduced him to the staff disparagingly as "Danny Boy". He assigned him to move appliances on the floor and straighten tires in the shop. Mister Dan told me he guessed this was some kind of initiation rite for apprentice managers. He could take a joke as well as the next guy, he thought. It'll change tomorrow, he reasoned.

But it didn't change. The next day simply brought on more of the same, and the next day, too. To add insult to injury, a salesman who reported to Mister Dan took to sarcastically referring to him as "Danny Boy" in the same mocking tone that the general manager had used when introducing him a few days earlier. His tormentor also refused to follow his directives, balked at every order, and generally made life miserable for Mister Dan. His self-confidence began to erode.

Over the next few weeks Mister Dan's boss did nothing about the abuses the rogue salesman heaped upon him, turning a blind eye to his constant insubordination. Meanwhile, Mister Dan was continually given menial tasks, those traditionally delegated to the hourly workers. He would come to work nattily dressed, only to be dispatched to do a job for which worn-out blue jeans and an old shirt would have been more suitable. All the while the irritating salesman, taking his cue from the dismissive boss, continued his barrage of verbal disdain directed toward Mister Dan. The increasingly open slights went virtually unchallenged by the gruff, seemingly uncaring crotchety old manager.

Mister Dan told me that he almost quit multiple times throughout the initial 90-day trial period. It was only sheer determination and an inborn streak of stubbornness that kept him from walking out on any given day. How dare anyone treat him so shabbily? He was a college graduate after all! He would one day be the CEO of the entire corporation, or so he thought. Who did this old duffer of a manager and his incompetent sidekick salesman think they were anyway?

The three-month marker was set to roll around. Hallelujah, thought Mister Dan, my time is up! I can escape this prison, this house of horrors, and move on to another company run by more reasonable and appreciative people. Someone else will certainly appreciate my great value, he told himself. He was consoled by the thought that the company leadership would one day see his picture on the cover of Forbes and wish they had treated him better.

Mister Dan could hardly wait for the ninetieth day. He fully intended to have his promised review, tell the manager what he thought of his antiquated management style, give the salesman an expletive-laced piece of his mind, and then walk out and take his expertise down the street to a far more progressive company. He would show them!

Well, the long awaited day finally arrived. It started uneventfully. He walked in the door, dressed nicely, but anticipating that he'd soon be dirty from some ridiculous assignment in the stock room that any junior clerk could carry out. So be it. He'd soon be free of this sweatshop he reasoned gloatingly.

Sure enough, the manager came toward him as soon as he walked in the door, with that look that affirmed he had a new torture in mind for the day. Mister Dan said he was steeled for whatever he dished out. In eight more hours this chapter of his life would be closed. He told himself that he could go through anything for just one more day.

At the very instant when the manager came within a couple of paces of him, Mister Dan said that his nemesis, the cheeky salesman, also walked by. "Hello, Danny Boy," he said sarcastically. "Going to unload another truck today? I hear it's scorching out there. Good luck! I'm going to be in here where the air conditioning is running full blast."

In a flash the manager turned on his heel, eyes narrowed, as he faced the passing salesman. "What did you just say to our fine assistant manager, to Mister Dan?" he asked angrily. "Don't you realize that today he is being promoted to full manager of his own store? How dare you speak to a distinguished manager of our chain in such a rude manner? You're fired for insubordination! Pack up and get out of here!"

According to Mister Dan, the salesman looked as though a bolt of lightning had hit him. The salesman stood there, mouth agape, unable to form words for several moments. Then, in a choked voice he sputtered to the manager, "But, sir, I've been talking to him like this for three months and you've never objected even once. Why the sudden change? Why are you letting me go after all of this time – when you said nothing for so long?"

"Well," said the manager, "I haven't liked your work or your general attitude for a long time. In fact, I was about to let you go back when Mister Dan showed up three months ago. Then I saw that you could help me solve a problem before I dismissed you. Back then Mister Dan was a gifted, but very cocky young man. I could see that he needed to be taken down a peg or two. I let you be the instrument to help him become more humble. And now that you've done that little job for me, goodbye! You're fired!"

By this point in Mister Dan's story I had finished my two donuts and most of my coffee. He stopped talking and looked straight at me for a half-minute or so. Moisture formed at the sides of his eyes – and in mine, too. I got it. The application of his true-to-life parable was not lost on me. Even though it wasn't needed he concluded with an interpretation to the story, one that I have never forgotten.

"Steve," he said, "I am not a very religious man. But I suspect you've needed to learn a few things that they couldn't teach you in seminary. Maybe God is using the pastor who is over you to teach you those lessons. He may not be the perfect instructor in your opinion, but if you quit you'll never know. Take it from a man who learned his lesson on the ninetieth day. Don't hand in that letter you wrote. It's up to you. Now let's get back to work. Oh, and no, I won't give you a fulltime job here if you quit the ministry. I won't be party to you escaping from God's call upon your life."

I called my wife and told her not to type the letter. I served under that senior pastor for another year before going on to graduate school. He seemed to become wiser in the last 12 months that I was with him! And to this day I thank God for Mister Dan and his lifesaving talk.

Extra-Milers learn to travel with opposition. The centurion we are helping isn't always kind and encouraging. But we know something he doesn't know, and probably never will. We know that persecution, however it may come, is often God's pathway to our growth. It may show up disguised as a sarcastic salesman or a critical boss. It takes several years and at least two miles to figure out this valuable truth.

In the meantime, please don't quit. The opposition we meet on the Extra Mile is more often than not for our benefit, however it may look at the time. So let's shoulder the centurion's pack with humility and move on. Promotion is on the way – if we don't quit too soon.

Chapter 16: Extra-Milers Walk Rather Than Run

"Jesus himself came up and walked along with them;
and they were kept from recognizing Him."
~ St. Luke

Secret # 16

It was the first Easter evening. The news had not yet circulated among the inner circle of disciples that Jesus had allegedly risen from the dead. Those who had heard the initial report were cynical. They had seen him die in a most gruesome and public manner just three days before. Any chance that he was alive now, after all of the bloodshed and mayhem of the crucifixion, was nil to none.

Pilate himself had signed the death certificate. The tomb had been sealed and carefully guarded since the execution. Jesus' cadre of followers would have given anything for him to be alive again, but they weren't going to be misguided any further. They had already wasted three years chasing what had now been proven to be another giant hoax.

And above all no one was prepared to believe the report of Mary of Magdela. She insisted that she had seen Jesus alive that very morning outside of his tomb. But then, Mary was consistently prone to exaggeration. There were some disciples who thought that they were idle tales. The confused and disappointed disciples weren't about to join in her hallucinations. Jesus was dead. They knew better. It was time to get on with life and making a living. Jesus wasn't coming back.

On that same Sunday afternoon two lesser-known disciples, one named Cleopas and one unnamed, set off for Emmaus, a village seven miles northwest of Jerusalem. Along the way they talked in hushed tones about what had happened over the course of the last week. It had been quite a study in extremes. Just a few days before they had followed behind a borrowed donkey upon which Jesus had made a magnificent entrance into the Holy City, heralding what many thought would be the end to Roman rule. The crowds had shouted themselves hoarse in loud adulation. Maybe this was the Messiah, they thought; the one who would send the hated Romans packing. Hosanna! Hosanna! Welcome, King Jesus!

But in less than a week it had somehow tragically all fallen apart. Some of the same voices that had cried praises the previous Sunday had shouted loudly in favor of a capital sentence for Jesus just as vociferously three days ago.

So now he was dead, quite dead, as were the hopes of a motley cast of assorted believers. These men and women had sacrificed three years of their lives in exchange for a dream that had become a nightmare. Most of the believers were reviewing their options and licking their wounds in a small out-of-the-way room on the second story of a nondescript Jerusalem house. For once, even Peter had little to say.

Meanwhile Cleopas and his companion had set off for Emmaus. As the two disciples conversed, a third man joined them. He seemed singularly uninformed about the topic of their discussion. Maybe he was from out of town. Many Jews from other lands came to Jerusalem each year for the days of Passover and were, therefore, unaware of the local news.

So the disciples filled the stranger in on what had occurred over the last few days. They summarized it quite well, telling him about the Sunday parade, the blowup with the religious leaders following the fracas at the Temple, the goodbye meal, the trial, and the subsequent execution of the young rabbi. They told the quiet pilgrim about Mary Magdalene's insistence that Jesus was alive again, come back from the dead as it were, and that she and some other disciples were saying he had sent a message to his followers about some kind of proposed reunion in Galilee within a few days.

When the disciples finished their summation they waited for the stranger to laugh at their account, especially the part about Mary's hallucination. But he didn't laugh. In fact, a slight smile danced on his lips and his eyes twinkled. If anything, he quietly sided with Mary, quoting from the Torah and a few of the ancient prophets to support the possibility that whoever the Messiah was, he would die and then somehow come to life again. Whose side was he on anyway, the two disciples wondered?

The shadows lengthened as they sauntered toward Emmaus. Time sped by and all too soon they found themselves at their destination. The stranger said his farewells and began to walk away from them toward an undisclosed spot out there beyond the village's limits. However, the disciples suddenly felt the nudge to invite the mysterious traveler to join them for their simple evening meal and perhaps to lodge with them for the night. It was, of course, the polite thing to do. Moreover there was something unfinished about the story that their guest had been telling them. They wanted to know the rest of the story. They longed for closure.

At first the stranger wasn't inclined to accept their invitation. He seemed bent on moving on. Nevertheless they persuaded him to stay and soon they were sitting at the supper table, with their mysterious guest leading them in a quiet prayer of thanksgiving for the food.

They would often recall in the years to come that his prayer, while simple, was powerful beyond any mealtime prayer they had ever heard. And as though anything could excel such passionate table grace, when they opened their eyes the pilgrim was no longer there. He had disappeared. And rushing in to fill the vacuum of his sudden departure came the acute awareness that the Magdalene woman was right after all. Jesus was alive! They had just walked and talked with him for the last couple of miles, somehow never suspecting his true identity.

Cleopas and his friend immediately headed back to Jerusalem. The night was young as they set out, but the darkness soon enveloped them completely, like a shroud. They intermittently trotted and loped back to the gathering place where the disciples had agreed to meet until the pressure from the Sanhedrin had lifted.

As they came near the outskirts of Jerusalem, they breathlessly reflected on how much running had taken place that day. Peter had run to the tomb in the morning. John, who was younger, had sprinted and surpassed Peter in the footrace to the sepulcher. And now Cleopas and his unnamed friend were moving as fast as their tired legs could carry them back to the Holy City and the possibility of arrest. But they were compelled to do it; the urgency of their message mandated haste and lack of caution.

So run they did, all the way up the steps to the upper room. They burst in unexpectedly on the cowering group of men, startling them and adding to their fear. No one could have known that these huddled few would soon courageously walk the length and breadth of the Roman Empire with the Good News that they were now about to receive.

Can we relate to those early disciples? In our culture many of us sit all day at work, and then run at sundown as a daily health regimen. Millions of us don athletic shoes and jogging gear for a power run around the neighborhood. We move from sedentary to sweaty, and then back again, with equal alacrity.

However, in days of yore transportation was readily available, but usually in the form of one's own two legs. Constant walking made additional exercise superfluous. Furthermore, why run and tire yourself out prematurely? The sensible thing to do was to stroll at a reasonable cadence. The sundial measured time in large increments. There were no watches with minute or second hands

Additionally, walking provided a wonderful excuse to chat with one's traveling companions. Indeed, did not the Shema of the Torah instruct elders to speak of holy things while walking? Some truths simply cannot be taught while sprinting. Walking provided the perfect setting to impart information and inspiration.

This is what happened on the first Easter evening. Jesus had nonchalantly sidled up to Cleopas and his companion on the road to Emmaus. Initially intent on merely getting from point A to point B, they were seriously considering the words they heard while enroute. Learning and walking proved to be a good combination. We miss a lot when we try to run to our own Emmaus. Life wasn't ever to be lived at a sprinting pace.

The Apostle Paul frequently refers to Christian discipleship as a walk, but never as a mad dash. Sins are typically extreme versions of thoughts or behaviors. The same thoughts or behaviors in proper moderation and within bounds are good. Thus, too often we either lazily loll about under a tree or, alternatively force ourselves to race pell-mell toward hell. Walking is the virtuous median point between insufficient and excessive movement.

Extra-Milers take the time to stroll through life. They take sacred moments to look others in the eye, listen to a friend (or foe) without interruption, and pause before answering a question. We should not be in such a hurry that we fail to stop for a meal and a prayer.

Years later, Cleopas and his companion would speak of their encounter on that road with reverence, in hushed tones. Someone had come alongside them and walked, talked, listened when it mattered most – and then disappeared. But though gone, he was certainly not forgotten. The world has been changed forever by the information that he shared on that trek.

Our slow and measured stride is not intended to be divisive or manipulative. The salesperson who takes the time to really hear what customers are saying has the greatest chance to gain a loyal following and become more successful. The manager, who walks beside those he or she serves, will gain far more than the boss who is a Type-A sprinter. And the fathers and mothers who slow down long enough to let the little legs of their children catch up to them, who take baby steps with them when necessary, who bend down to eye level to give or receive a hug, will one day be made proud by their appreciative brood.

Every year or so I take some friends and parishioners to the ancient Promised Land. I jokingly forewarn my fellow travelers that while Jesus covered Israel during three years of ministry, we will have just ten days to trace his steps. The mantra for our trip: "We will run where Jesus walked!" They laugh. And run we do, from Dan to Beersheba.

Is there ever a time for haste in life, we ask? Certainly. High speed is required at times. Cleopas and his friend probably made the return journey to Jerusalem very rapidly. Easter was a day of rapid movement and even today such urgency is required occasionally. But the cheetah doesn't unceasingly sprint across the Serengeti simply because it can. Running through life can be a great adrenaline rush. However, in the end the rat race just turns us into faster rats.

At such moments, it behooves us to reflect on the words of architect Mies Van Der Rohe: "Less is more." Put aside the cell phone for a day. Get on an airplane without benefit of headphones plugged into each ear. Go on vacation without each day being packed with theme parks and tourist meccas. Give customers your undivided attention and put aside the remote control in favor of a conversation.

In a word: Walk! Jesus did. We have no record of the Master racing anywhere. He walked to Lazarus' tomb. He walked along the Via Dolorosa. He walked with a couple of ordinary people all the way to Emmaus. And he will walk with you and me – if we slow down enough to keep pace and listen to what he has to say. In so doing he'll give us the strength to go the Extra Mile, a power that speed demons seldom possess, having expended their resources on attaining the unremarkable end of the first mile as quickly as possible.

Extra-Milers saunter because they must ultimately go further. They pace themselves, not for the easy first mile, but for the more strenuous second mile. So, my fellow pilgrims let us walk in lockstep with the stranger on the Road to Emmaus – throughout this day, this year, this life, and on into the next.

Remember, let's walk rather than run.

Chapter 17: Extra-Milers Willingly Put Their Lives on the Line

"Greater love has no one than this, that he lay down
his life for his friends."
~ Jesus

Secret # 17

In 1962, when I was thirteen, my father accepted the assignment to be the director of a ministerial training institute in a suburb of Buenos Aires, Argentina. The school was housed in the former German ambassador's residence, a place that still gave broad hints of its Nazi ties less than two decades before. For example, among other things a large black-and-white marble swastika had to be dug up from the cellar floor before the school's dedication ceremonies. Our home, which adjoined the campus, was on Calle Garibaldi, a street in a community across town made infamous by Adolph Eichmann's capture there just a short time before we had arrived.

One day I noticed an elderly little lady walking across the seminary grounds in the company of my father. Later I asked him who she was. He replied that she was a woman who had suffered greatly during the Holocaust. She had lost family members in a concentration camp and had barely escaped with her own life. A hero of sorts, she had come to speak at the school and had signed one of her books especially for me. I could barely make out her scrawl in red ink on the cover page. I finally deciphered it: Corrie ten Boom, it read with the added notation of a scripture verse below her signature – 2 Corinthians 4: 6, 7.

I so wish I had known who she was back then and all about how she had put herself in harm's way during World War II, all to save 800 Jews from almost certain extermination. I was made aware of her huge sacrifice only when I saw the movie "The Hiding Place" many years later, which very movingly documented her willingness to put her life on the line for voiceless people during the Nazi regime. I have thought of her many times since, especially when walking by the tree planted in her memory at the Vad Yashem Memorial in Jerusalem. And when I am in Jerusalem I usually go by the Catholic cemetery on Mount Zion, to lay a stone on the tomb of Oskar Schindler, who was also in Argentina for a short time after the war. It took another film, Schindler's List, to inform millions of us of Oskar's heroism on behalf of the 1200 Jews he saved during the mid-1940s. It is true that Mr. Schindler was a womanizer, an unrepentant rascal and a chronic alcoholic. Yet he was also a genuine hero. Make no mistake about it.

I've reluctantly come to the conclusion that those who put their lives on the line for others don't always emerge well when scrutinized too closely. I leave it to God to make all final judgments, but in this life some Extra-Milers tend to have warts and scars. Such people aren't always attractive when observed under a microscope. Still, I daresay that heroic individuals with alarming imperfections are to be preferred over more attractive do-nothings who shrink and shirk in the hour of crisis.

Some time back I had the opportunity to hear Paul Rusesabagina, the real life manager of the infamous Hotel Rwanda, tell of his involvement in saving 1268 lives during the days of his country's 1994 genocide. In unadorned English, with the cautious vocabulary of one speaking a second language, he told of the brutality of those days when 800,000 innocents were sacrificed in a few months to the gods of vengeance and mayhem. He remarked several times during the course of his address that what he had done was nothing particularly noble. He was, after all, "just a hotel manager doing his job – that of taking care of people."

I've met some good hotel managers in my time. They may have given me an upgrade to a mini-suite or expedited laundry service. On a couple of occasions I even got a free night or two out of the deal. But none of them ever risked their earthly existence to ward off machete wielding thugs, still drenched in the blood of their recent victims. That is more than four-star service, I say, far more.

Perhaps you've heard the story of the chicken and the pig reading an advertisement plastered on a rural billboard beside a roadside cafe. The sign said: "Eat ham and eggs here each morning." The chicken commented on the reasonableness of the suggestion. The pig, on the other hand, was horrified at the idea.

"What's your objection?" asked the chicken.

"Well," said the pig, "it's like this: For you it is merely a token contribution, whereas for me and my fellow swine it means total sacrifice."

Zig Ziglar said that "some people have the commitment level of a kamikaze pilot on his 28th mission." We envision ourselves as heroes in the abstract, but emerge less well in the harsh glare of the noonday sun. In my opinion, that's what often happens when there is a hit-and-run accident. Frequently the runaway driver has made a lifestyle of avoidance in little things. So, when it comes time to own up to a major issue the automatic course of action is to run and hide. I can say with certainty that such a person would not have saved a Jew in Nazi Germany or have negotiated for a fellow Rwandan to be spared from execution by a hotel swimming pool in Kigali.

Just before Jesus was betrayed by Judas in the Garden of Gethsemane all of his disciples had professed their willingness to die for him. They had vowed that they would protect him at all costs. But when the time came for deeds to match creeds some of them fled. Three years of following Jesus, hearing his sermons and seeing his miracles, made little difference. It was every man for himself. ("Master? What master? I don't even know the fellow!")

Of course, we would have done differently, right? But are we bolder than the disciples? Would we have behaved like Corrie or Oskar or Paul if given the chance? Or would we have chosen anonymity at the least and collusion at the most? The true and honest answer is found in our noblest responses to the seemingly insignificant decisions of life.

Fred Craddock once preached that we all dream of giving a million-dollar check to charity one day, in a giant lump sum, in front of God and the whole world. But, he added, most of us must content ourselves with giving a number of much smaller checks – one hundred and three dollars here, two dollars and forty-eight cents there – checks that may one day many years from now, when we are old and gray, add up to the full million. Such cumulative charity is not flashy and will garner little public acclaim. But it shall be noticed someday by the One to whom it matters most. A million is a million, whether given all at once before flashing cameras or over a lifespan in relative obscurity.

And thus it is with the way we put our lives on the line. Few of us will have the chance to literally save a life. If we are waiting for the klieg lights and a hero's parade we may wait for a long time. But this should not keep us from doing a small courageous deed here; writing a letter to the editor there; partnering in a protest elsewhere; constantly risking humiliation by being willing to do the right (even if unpopular) thing everywhere. It is in this manner that our numerous small "checks" are written to both God and society. Thus we put our lives on the line incrementally; always prepared for the ultimate sacrifice should it ever become necessary.

Have you heard of Kitty Genovese? She was a 28-year old girl from Queens who was brutally murdered in the wee hours of March 13, 1964 within earshot of 38 indifferent people. The almost unbelievable outcome is that no one called the police!

(Well, one did call the authorities, but agonized so long over the decision that Kitty had died of her wounds by the time the police arrived.)

The 38 witnesses, when interviewed by the reporters and sociologists, who were looking for answers to the uncaring non-responsiveness, repeatedly said much the same thing: "We didn't want to get involved."

In a crisis a person normally goes through three stages while moving from passivity to practical involvement. First, there must be information. We cannot respond to what we don't know or understand. Of course, as demonstrated by the case of Kitty Genovese, facts don't always lead to further action. But without information one will not progress to the second stage: Inspiration.

Inspiration is the fuel that propels us to get involved. This motivation comes, not from the head, but from the heart. Mere intellect won't make one willing to hide a Jew or defend at Tutsi. Inspiration is a visceral response. It is a reflexive action, almost like breathing or blinking.

If the information gets to our brains and souls, unless we turn our heads and stop our ears, we will be compelled to act. Let's call that transformation. Information, inspiration, and transformation add up to action, if we have established a track record for standing up and speaking out before the moment of crisis. If our style has been to run away or put blinders on, we'll pretend nothing has happened or we'll skew the facts to conform to what we want to see and hear. It is then and there that the saddest and most repulsive events of history repeat themselves.

I was at the Vad Yashem Memorial just outside of Jerusalem several years ago. The memorial is partly a museum, partly an indictment, and partly a warning. The buildings and grounds are dedicated to keeping alive the memory of the many Jewish lives lost in the Nazi Holocaust before a watching world. I have been there numerous times and it never fails to move me. It is a place that poses far more questions than it does answers.

I was at the museum yet again, pausing at the last exhibit in bewilderment. I was pondering about how this savage event could ever have occurred under the gaze of apparently civilized people, while other nations contributed to the crime by looking away. Behind me stood a kindly German lady with her granddaughter, a fact I deduced from their conversation. With exceptional tenderness the matronly old woman whispered within my hearing to the child, "Now my dear, I have brought you here as you asked me to do. But as Grandma has told you many times, none of this ever truly happened. It is a made up story. Pay no attention to it and don't let it bother you. There, there, now. Don't cry."

If we treat information with disdain there can be and will be no inspiration. And most certainly there will be no incarnation. No valiant actions will follow. The turning of our heads can shut out a holocaust. Changing a word like genocide into a more acceptable phrase like "acts of genocide", as was the case in Rwanda, lets life and death go on without anyone feeling the worse for either one.

It is this same claim to ignorance that doesn't see the homeless, the disenfranchised, the poorer, the smaller and the least.

The final stage is involvement. This is where Mercy Avenue and Main Street intersect. It is when you are ready to stand, all by yourself if need be, in front of a tank in Tiananmen Square. It is when you are prepared to put your career on the line because a person is being sexually harassed at work and no one will speak up, except you. It is when you are a popular party politician, facing an easy reelection campaign, but a hard moral decision that could potentially transform you into an unemployed statesman stands in opposition to your conscience.

There are many ways to be a martyr. Not all of them are fatal or final. Sometimes it is about living with the knowledge that you did the right thing, whatever the price, rather than dying one day in a comfy bed with a soiled, compromised set of values as your final bedfellow. Putting one's life on the line need not mean that one's life must end literally, as Corrie and Oskar and Paul and others prove – for in their cases they all lived on when they might have died. Our figurative death comes in the willingness to sacrifice if need be, not always in its literal actualization.

Whether or not we lose our job or our prestige or even our life is in the hands of the One who really knows what putting one's life on the line is all about. He once looked around a table at twelve headstrong, cocksure friends. He made a powerful declaration in such a quiet voice that they missed the point, at least that particular night. "Greater love," he said, "has no one than this that he lay down his life for his friends."

Extra-Milers have all heard these words before. Many have been called upon to live them out – and some even to die. All of us will be called upon to do one or the other sometime, someplace before life is over. Let us prepare for that day, being ever vigilant lest we find ourselves at the moment of truth fleeing, stumbling back toward the single mile marker of shame and mediocrity.

Extra-Milers put their lives on the line – the Extra Mile line.

MILE 2

Chapter 18: Extra-Milers Take Derision in Stride

"When Jesus left there, the Pharisees and the
teachers of the law began to oppose him fiercely..."
~ St. Luke

Secret # 18

In biblical times going the Extra Mile had its downside. Not everyone was sold on the idea. The Jewish zealots saw the practice as an unnecessary concession to their Roman invaders. The Romans, on the other hand, like schoolyard bullies got the feeling that a person willing to go beyond duty's call was an easy mark for open ridicule and even further abuse. How could the disciples of Rabbi Jesus strike a reasonable balance? Should they bargain for a mile and a half – you know the age-old old "split the difference" ploy?

I recall seeing an old black-and-white episode of Candid Camera. It featured an assembly line at a large commercial bakery where pies were being made. The workers didn't know it, but someone behind the scenes was speeding up the conveyor belt. All the while a hidden camera was capturing the humorous human responses to this phenomenon.

The reactions were rather evenly divided. One group worked faster and harder, comically trying unsuccessfully to put the decorative sprinkles and whipped cream atop the pies as they sped by, doing their best to avoid losing the pastries in their care. But in short order the pies began to fly off the end of the assembly line to the horror and consternation of the more diligent of the workers. They had tried and failed. Most looked crestfallen at the waste. The company's loss was their loss, too.

However, the larger segment of the pie-makers took the maniacal conveyor belt in stride. They made an initial less-than-heroic stab at saving some of the errant pies, but soon resorted to calmly watching them fall onto the floor with a smirk and a sigh. They oozed a "hey, why try, after all, it's not my loss" attitude.

I still remember the rather bored looks on their faces, looks I have seen on the countenances of many workers across the world. It essentially conveyed the attitude, "I'm a one-mile person and I dare you to make me go a step further than what is required."

Such an entrenched mentality will seldom welcome the go-getter's philosophy of life. If we intend to excel at an endeavor, we must be prepared to encounter the criticism of a mob of one-milers. The care-less rabble will fight those who try valiantly to persuade them that the Extra Mile is a desirable destination. They would rather see the pies fall on the floor than try harder.

Five of my teen years were lived in Argentina. One of my Argentine friends was named Alfredo, a fair-skinned lad of

Spanish decent with a penchant for making machines from scratch. My friends and I often mocked his efforts, urging him to leave his obsession with cogs and pulleys to play soccer or go swimming with us instead. Even on the rare occasions when he gave in, even while kicking the ball or sunbathing he continued to talk incessantly about some machine or other that he was assembling. It was a mild irritation to those of us who were far more devoted to run-of-the-mill youthful pursuits – like girls, and sports, and pizza.

Alfredo's favorite project was "el projector", or the projector. He was determined to make a sixteen-millimeter movie projector from spare parts he had found or purchased from a parts store with his meager allowance. Alfredo babbled about the progress of his pet project so much so that we began to tune him out.

When his weekly reports became even more unbearable, we would dunk him in the pool or give him a good-natured roughing-up. Not to be dissuaded, he would emerge from any of our forms of good-natured punishment spouting the virtues of some obscure part that was going to soon find its way into "la maquina".

I left Argentina and the projector still wasn't completed. For a while Alfredo and I corresponded but, as we are all prone to do in time, it soon was out of sight and out of mind. I would occasionally think of my friend and his compulsion to finish his machine and wondered if he had finally succeeded. Then I forgot about it altogether.

A quarter of a century passed and I unexpectedly had reason to visit Argentina again. I made plans to reconnect with some of my old friends and classmates, one of them being Alfredo. After going through a number of contacts I was able to obtain his unpublished phone number and I gave him a call. He offered to pick me up and take me to the Costanera, the riverfront on the Rio de la Plata known for its many restaurants featuring succulent Argentine beef.

Alfredo picked me up in his new car. He was dressed to the nines. His lovely wife was by his side. The nerdy plastic pocket protector of his youth was gone as was the slide rule and the pockets crammed with bits of paper on which were scribbled proposed improvements to his sacrosanct "projector". Alfredo was the personification of a man who had become a success by way of the Extra Mile.

Over supper I asked him about the projector. Whatever happened to it? He laughed and said, "Oh, that! Why I finally completed it, but when I plugged it in the thing caught on fire and burned up!" Then he gave a wistful smile and continued, "It was then and there, when the machine that I had devoted so much time and money to was still in flames, that I knew I wanted to be an engineer. It is to that moment and God that I owe all I now am."

Argentina was in the midst of a recession but my old friend had plenty. His job was secure. Why? It went back to a defining epoch in his life when he had decided to put aside the friendly opposition of good-natured friends to pursue a dream; to build something he saw as meaningful; to meet an elusive goal. Even when mocked he wouldn't give up his Extra Mile aspirations.

Be assured of this: If ever you attempt anything of significance there will be a chorus of dissenters chanting negative intonations in your ears. Their song will most often have three verses, the first two in a minor key: You can't do it, you won't do it, and (when you finally succeed) I knew you could do it! Criticism has no favorite century or nationality. Anytime and anyplace will do nicely.

But just remember: Premature predictions of failure will turn into flattery because you will have managed to prove them wrong. Criticism is the toll one pays to walk the second, the longer, the Extra Mile.

Is the additional fee worth it? It ultimately paid off for Alfredo and, I suspect, it will for you and me, too. Granted, that's just my opinion. You'll never know for sure until you try it for yourself.

Here comes a Roman soldier calling your name right now. What are you going to do? Think – quickly! You can control the distance of the enforced first mile walk but, more importantly, it is within your gift to control your attitude if you choose to go the Extra Mile.

The question that you and I must answer is simple: Will it be one mile – or two? A bit of derision awaits you if you select the Extra Mile, but you will profit from it. Consider Alfredo and his projector. We laughed at him then, but now he's the one laughing – laughing all the way to the bank!

Chapter 19: Extra-Milers Welcome Necessary Change

"But I tell you the truth: It is for your good that I am
going away."
~ Jesus

Secret # 19

Life, when reduced to its simplest terms, is a series of interconnected changes. Like a long train with many boxcars, our years on the planet are comprised of multiple experiences joined together, spanning the tracks from the past to the present and beyond.

It is my observation that how a person manages change determines, to a great extent, the level of success or failure in life. Those who roll with the punches and don't fight the riptide tend to survive, even thrive, in the midst of chaos. But the ones who stiffen up in anticipation of the blows that life delivers so adroitly, who refuse to be elastic when the unexpected appears, frequently fare poorly in the end.

The problem, of course, is that most of us don't enjoy or welcome change. Our bodies strive for homeostasis, the maintenance of the body's status quo. For example, we anatomically try to maintain a body temperature of 98.6 degrees Fahrenheit. We drink liquids, put on and take off clothes, and go through assorted gyrations to stay as near to this ideal body temperature as possible.

Homeostasis seems to be the human goal psychologically and spiritually as well. We feel comfortable with routine. There is predictability in driving to work along the same route each day. Yes, we complain about the potholes. "Why doesn't someone do something about the condition of these roads?" we ask. But when the road crew puts up detour signs and forces us to go to work another way while the desired repairs are being made, we don't like the temporary change, even if it results in ultimate improvement.

When we go to church we instinctively migrate to the same pew. A pox on the person who takes our favorite spot! We can cope with computers that become obsolete in six months, yet find ourselves drawn to return to the same vacation cabin again and again. Why? The answer is simply that we don't readily embrace change. Breaking out of routine is viewed as a necessary evil, not as a warm and fuzzy friend.

Once I was on an overseas trip and my luggage was lost for a full week. Normally finicky about my attire, I surprised myself by how quickly I adjusted to a reduced wardrobe that was made up of just a few items I had picked up along the way. But I went into serious withdrawal over my missing French coffee press, the canister of Arabica coffee beans I had packed, and the morning ritual of making and consuming my own black java. Some things we dare not change or we become agitated and insecure.

A couple I knew had a problem with their three-year-old son. Every night at about midnight the toddler would come into their room and crawl into bed with them until morning. This was inconvenient on many levels. So they came up with a brilliant plan.

The child's birthday was only a couple of weeks away. They began to make a great deal about the upcoming celebration they were planning for him. He would soon be four years old, a big boy. On that day, they told him, he'd receive many gifts that only "older" children were allowed to have. What defined an "older" child? Well, coincidentally one who did not sleep with his father and mother any longer!

They repeatedly explained to the lad that after his birthday party he would need to sleep in his own room, with his newly acquired grown up toys, as all bigger children do. There wouldn't be any more slipping into mom and dad's bed in the middle of the night. It wouldn't be proper for a "grown up" four-year-old boy to behave in such a manner. With maturity would come the need for responsibility and courage. Did he understand his new assignment? Of course he did, he replied.

So, the birthday party came and went. The candles were blown out, the gifts were opened, and soon it was bedtime. The newly-turned-four-year-old boy went to his bed surrounded on all sides by his new cache of toys and video games. He seemed so content nestled there among them. His parents turned out the light and tiptoed out of the room, breathing a collective sigh of relief. They were finally going to get a full night to themselves.

But, lo and behold, just when everything was going so well the child strolled into their room at midnight with his blanket in tow. He hopped into their bed like he had in the past. My friend and his wife weren't amused. With much less patience than in bygone days they firmly explained to him that he was a big kid now, as evidenced by his fourth birthday party and his many big-boy gifts. Sleeping with his parents was no longer part of the deal. To this logic he replied: "I've thought it over and I don't want to be big after all. You can have the toys back. I want to come in here with you every night and sleep in your bed with you guys, forever and ever!"

No, we don't like change, not at four and not at 40.

In John's Gospel we have the record of a discussion Jesus had with his disciples the night he was put to death. The occasion was at the Passover meal, which was usually a joyous, boisterous event. But no one in the room was in celebration mode as the unleavened bread made its rounds. The room was thick with the almost-tangible atmosphere of impending change. The disciples sensed that something big would soon occur and it wasn't going to be good. They could feel it hanging in the air over the table. And it would most likely mean that things would never be the same again.

Jesus was making some rather abstract comments about "going away and their not seeing him anymore". The message was muddled even more by a collective sense of denial that emanated from the twelve. It sounded like their beloved Rabbi was saying goodbye when he had barely said hello. If this happened there would be no more private teaching times, no further miracles, no laughs by the campfire, and they would lose the respect now afforded them when they followed their popular leader into a new village.

By closing their ears to the message of change on that night they missed the portion of the Master's talk that had to do with the benefits of his departure. Had they listened more carefully they could have spared themselves the embarrassing spate of denials and betrayals that would come later that evening, and even on into the next day. They would have heard him say that what was about to occur was for their own good. They would have been open to the upside rather than the downside of the message the Master was trying to convey.

Let's face the facts: Change is difficult. Who willingly wants to move out of his or her comfort zone? That's why the Extra Mile fails to immediately appeal to most hikers. Going two miles instead of one requires a transformational shift of heart and mind. It isn't merely a slight midcourse correction. It's a fresh paradigm; an entirely new template.

As a result we tend to avoid such change at all costs, even to the extent of "giving back the toys" and staying immature forever. We prefer to tightly hug the known rather than risk embracing the unknown. Change is the unknown. For too many of us, dragons lurk beyond the safe, fully explored areas of our lives. We have been taught that the earth is flat and we don't want to challenge tightly held assumptions, even when there is ample evidence to prove them wrong.

Of course, some realities may force us to change: The pink slip, the call from the highway patrol, the hurricane, or the economy. These circumstances all come into our lives unbidden. The death of a loved one is the ultimate potential change foisted upon the unsuspecting. Elisabeth Kubler-Ross documents five stages the living go through in dealing with the impending death of a relative or friend with a terminal disease: Denial, anger, bargaining, depression and, finally, acceptance.

Few of the living or the dying passively face the ultimate change called death, whatever our brand of theology. It isn't a matter of cowardice, but it is an instinctive resistance to change that compels most of us to grip the safety-handles of this life with white knuckles rather than letting go. Even those who profess that heaven is for real pray passionately that they won't be called upon to go there until the last drop of life has been squeezed from their mortal frames. We are prepared to go one day, just not this day.

Yet, change is inevitable. The unexpected must and will happen. We can only decide to accept or resist the process. The dynamic equivalent of a 21st century centurion calls us out of the orderliness of our well-planned day to carry his pack for one mile. We can chafe or grow during the enforced walk, but walk we must. If we feel abused because the event wasn't in our plans, if we resent the intruder who has bullied his way into our schedule, then the second sacrificial mile will not be a consideration when we finish the first obligatory mile. We will lose out because the abundant life doesn't become exciting or risky or successful until we have passed the threshold that leads to the Extra Mile.

The disciples were informed of the change that would occur, but they weren't given a vote about whether or not they thought it was a good idea. There was no referendum; no opinion poll. In one sense Judas voted by becoming a traitor to the cause. He is forever remembered as the one who didn't even finish the first furlong, not to speak of the first mile. When events and the person he was following didn't fit his plans any longer he walked out into the darkness of the night. Ironically, the other disciples thought he had exited to feed the poor. They mistakenly thought he was an Extra Mile change agent when the only thing "extra" about him was that he was two-faced, a double agent out only for himself, and a small shell of a man with an extra-large ego. There have been no accolades for Judas for 21 long centuries. Judas wanted nothing to do with positive change. To be fair, neither did the other disciples. However, they stayed around long enough to learn this lesson: Change, more often than not, is an opportunity rather than a curse.

What Jesus said came true. His departure ushered in a new opportunity for all concerned. The Spirit came, an event that could not have happened without Jesus' departure. The curtain had to descend on Act One before Act Two could commence. History bears witness to the veracity of Jesus' proposition.

Change is most often the best thing that can happen to us, resist it though we may.

A Chinese parable tells of an old man who lived with his son on a farm. One night the man's only horse ran away. His neighbors came to console him on his misfortune. He asked them, "How do you know this is misfortune?"

A week later the horse returned bringing with it a herd of wild horses. The neighbors gathered again, this time to congratulate the farmer on his good luck. The old man smiled and said: "How do you know this is good fortune?"

A short time later the man's son was trying to break one of the wild stallions and it broke him instead. His leg was badly injured. The neighbors came yet again to comfort the father. "But," protested the father, "how do you know with certainty that this is so evil? Be patient. Wait for the final outcome."

A few months passed and an army captain came to conscript the son to fight in a brutal war. But the son was not drafted because of his limp. He went on to live while others died. Again the community gathered to praise the family's fortune. The father responded as he had in the past: "Who knows what this change really means? We must not fight it. We must not call it good or bad merely because it is welcome or unwelcome. Wait and see. It will work out."

Ultimately, positive change wins out. And in the process it won't alter or modify timeless principles. Some things don't change, shouldn't change. In a house you can move certain walls with no ill effect, but you'd better not touch the ones that provide structural support. King Solomon put it another way: "Don't move the ancient boundary stones."

A business can change its products to adapt to the market, but should never change its high ethical standards. In the midst of change some things mustn't change. Middle C is middle C, whether the musical genre is jazz, rock, gospel, or classical. The Extra-Miler will become adept at recognizing what is negotiable and what is not, while striving all the while to go twice as far as the norm along the road of permissible change.

Ask a caterpillar if it wants to become a butterfly and, if caterpillars could talk, it would probably say no. Why not? Because a homely caterpillar fails to make a connection between itself and the beautiful butterfly hovering above a nearby flower. It prefers not to become a chrysalis. It would sooner stay as it is, a mere worm wiggling clumsily along a branch, than to risk it all on transformation brought on by metamorphosis.

Extra Mile people welcome necessary change, not because it is easy but because it is hard. It is the only way to ultimately excel. There is no virtue in remaining the same, even as there is no reward for changing just for change's sake alone.

Any person can walk one mile with a frown on his face and a resentful attitude, bearing the heavy pack of the whistling Roman soldier. Only those who welcome change can envision a paradigm that exceeds the minimum and moves well beyond existing boundaries. I suspect you are one of them.

So, let's not get too comfortable. We need to keep moving and changing while always heading toward the ultimate goal. Necessary change is good.

That's why we need to celebrate the ever-changing terrain of our journey. Life only truly becomes extraordinary when we change by adding the extra, Extra Mile that is.

MILE 2

Chapter 20: Extra-Milers Are Truthful Without Being Unkind

"You are right when you say you have no husband.
The fact is, you have had five husbands, and the man
you now have is not your husband. What you have
just said is quite true."
~ Jesus speaking to a Samaritan woman

Secret # 20

Quite often, on my way home from a speaking engagement, I ask my wife, "So, how did I do?" She could easily reply, "You went way too long" or "The story about the man and the elephant made no sense". But we haven't been married for over four decades without learning a thing or two about each other. In other words, she knows that at that moment I'm usually not inviting a serious critique, but fishing for a compliment. I want to hear something approximating, "You hit it out of the park, hon!"

And when she comes into the room in a new outfit after shopping all day, spins around and arches an inquiring eyebrow, what comes out of my mouth had better not be, "Where did you get that thing?" Even if there is a flaw in the pattern, it isn't her color, or the style makes her look a bit like a mature pom-pom girl I had best set such commentary aside until a more opportune time. She wants me to smile approvingly and murmur that it appears to be tailor-made just for her.

Don't get me wrong, truth certainly needs to be told. However, the when, where, what, and how of truth telling needs to be considered carefully before giving full expression to an opinion. A person who perpetually says, "To be perfectly honest" probably wonders why he or she has few friends. Even in youth we learn to balance honesty with other prevailing factors. What we can say and what we should reveal are always at odds with each another. Full disclosure must have its day, but perhaps it shouldn't be this day. There is time and place for candor, and this may not be the time or place.

Indeed, on the Extra Mile journey we all need to balance total transparency with timely wisdom. It isn't a bad idea to occasionally have an unexpressed thought, especially if we intend to travel the Extra Mile road in harmony with our hiking companions. The longer the potential journey, the more we should consider this maxim. The timing of one's transparency is arguably as important as the content of the opinion itself.

However, there inevitably comes a time when we should be up-front with our fellow travelers. The misplaced or misunderstood joke in the sermon needs to be discussed so the message can be improved the next time it is delivered. The unflattering dress should be returned in favor of one more suited to the wearer of the garment. The unexplained outburst of anger can be broached with a sympathetic, "Is everything okay?"

There is a time for every purpose under heaven, including truth telling. Truth, when spoken kindly and at the right moment, leads to liberation and improvement. If we can learn to pick the correct moment to unveil truth we will have learned another valuable Extra Mile trait. The truth does, indeed, set all of us free – if the revelation is both gentle and well timed. When the hearers are convinced that we have their best interest at heart, they are usually receptive. The co-workers who know we have their backs are more likely to listen to another point of view.

Jesus was going through Samaria with his disciples. It was closing in on midday. The Master and his men stopped by a well at high noon, but they had no bucket to put down into the well. So while his followers went to get a bite of lunch, Jesus chatted with a local woman who had providentially come to draw water at that unusual hour.

A respectable woman of that era would not typically be doing her chores at noon unless she had a night job and tended to sleep in. Since there were no second and third shifts in the pre-industrial world many have assumed that the woman's evening activities were of a questionable sort. As a result, no self-respecting Jewish teacher of the law would be caught near such a woman, much less engage in meaningful dialogue with her. That she was a vilified Samaritan made conversation with her even more socially unlikely.

However, Jesus was not your ordinary rabbi. So, they talked and talked some more, the loose woman and the soft-spoken teacher. They chatted about the merits of limpid water when thirsty, the history of the well around which they now sat, and how that both water and thirst can be metaphors for unsatiated spiritual longings. Then Jesus casually asked her to go call her husband. He wanted to meet him, he said.

To Jesus' request the unnamed woman flippantly remarked that she had no husband. This reply was technically true. Although the Samaritan lady had been married five times, she was presently involved in a live-in relationship without "benefit of clergy", to put it delicately. Hence, she was legally single. However, Jesus felt the need to confront her deception. He did so, not to show off his prophetic powers, but to ultimately give her a full measure of the liberty she had bypassed throughout her entire dysfunctional life.

Ever so gently he reminded her of the truth and nudged her toward giving it a voice. One might say that she hadn't been very successful as a spouse, having been married five times. She needed to acknowledge that fact, not as punishment, but as the first step along her own Extra Mile journey. Her marital record, while abysmal, did not cause Jesus to care for her any less; the Master knew her failings, but he loved her still. His expectation of full disclosure from her wasn't a punishment for her sins, but a remedy for what ailed her. He wasn't rubbing it in; he was rubbing it out!

Virtue is the median point between the two extremes. On one hand honesty can be brutal if it isn't mixed with love when delivered. On the other hand, isn't a disinclination to confront ultimately a toxic denial of facts and feelings? Neither extreme is healthy or holy. Both are characteristics of those who are content with the simplicity of single-mile relationships. Only truth can set us free.

When you intend to take only a short walk, there is no need to be revelational with the centurion who strides at your side. After all, you plan to dump the backpack and the backpack's owner at the first mile marker anyway. So, why engage in the messiness of interpersonal bonding, which includes a certain degree of forthrightness? Being upfront with an ancient Roman soldier or a modern-day peer is exceedingly risky.

The uncomplicated relationship, while short and shallow, is maintenance-free. Why be truthful when you plan to part company at the first opportunity? Talk about the weather, sports, or fashions and let it go at that.

Being an Extra-Miler requires a special brand of "kind honesty". The Apostle Paul championed truth spoken in love. It would behoove us all to read 1 Corinthians 13 anew and continue to do so as a regular exercise. Pure love isn't easily riled nor is it inclined to point out every little deficiency in one's companions on the Extra Mile road. Truth telling is not the same as nitpicking.

We must have governors and limits on what we share lest our honesty become a bone of contention. If you have ever walked the trail with people who feel God put them on the planet to be in charge of global quality control then you know what I mean. In another teaching venue Jesus chides the one whom, while having a large pole firmly stuck in his own eye, has his tweezers ready to remove the speck of dust from another's cornea.

The only people Jesus was deliberately unkind to were the religious leaders of the day. He wasted no time getting to the heart of the matter with the scribes and teachers of the law. He called them snakes, pointed out their bad manners in public, mocked their pomposity, and had no trouble naming names.

Jesus refused to stand on ceremony with those who voted to exclude lepers, who were the first to gather rocks to stone wayward women, and who thought of themselves as morally superior to the rest of the world. For such people he reserved a cut-to-the-chase level of truth telling that belied the kindness he showed those mired in their openly acknowledged folly. After all, he had come to heal those who knew they were sick – and to straightjacket those who relied on their own righteousness for salvation.

There are times when we are obliged to tell our traveling companions the unwelcome truth, but we must do it ever so kindly. "No, the dress does not look good on you. Yes, the message was too long. Sue, you have a drinking problem. Jimmy, you didn't make the team. You have cancer. It isn't working out. We must cut the budget. There will be no Florida vacation this year." Truth and kindness, when taken in equal and simultaneous doses, help make the medicine go down.

It is a challenge to know how to deliver truth; honest interchange is more of an art than a science. Jesus was the expert at delivering facts without needlessly hurting feelings. He never was unkind without intentionality. If he spoke truth it was invariably seasoned with kindness, with the lone exception of the words he directed toward those who used their own brand of frankness like an indiscriminate axe rather than a precise scalpel.

The woman at the well ran to tell the entire village about her conversation with the pilgrim who had asked her for a midday glass of water. Who knows how far it was back to the town: One mile, maybe two? She told her neighbors, and perhaps her latest paramour, that she had finally met a person who was both truthful and kind. In response to her news she brought an entire crowd back with her to the well. They didn't come to drive the prophet away. They came to ask him to stay for two more days; to walk with them for two more miles; to reveal to them their innermost hurts and failings as long as it was done with kindness.

Those whose backpacks we are assigned to help carry along the road of life do not generally object to candor as long as it is intermingled with thoughtfulness. The most difficult truth can be conveyed honestly when accompanied by tears in the eyes and compassion in the heart. Let's resolve to improve the way we deliver the truth as we attempt to help those with whom we stride, ever forward and onward.

Let's mix straight talk with saving grace as we traverse the pathway we all now have come to call the Extra Mile.

Chapter 21: Extra-Milers Get Up When They Fall Down

Going a little farther, he fell to the ground and
prayed that if possible the hour might pass from him.
"Abba, Father," he said, "Everything is possible for
you. Take this cup from me. Yet not what I will, but
what you will." Then he returned to his disciples and
found them sleeping.
~ Jesus in the Garden of Gethsemane

Secret # 21

Here's a guarantee: If you are a hiker, you will most assuredly trip and fall from time to time. Age doesn't matter. Toddlers stumble hundreds of times in the course of learning to walk. School age kids trip and are often bruised in the midst of their childhood games and everyday activities. Adults move more slowly and thus may fall less readily, but even they take a misstep now and then. Anyone who walks will fall multiple times throughout his or her lifetime. Stumbling is a given, a constant reminder of our flawed human condition. The only variable is whether or not we will get up after we take a spill.

So, if you don't want to risk hitting the dirt, then stay in your easy chair or don't move from the sofa. Be inactive. Play it safe. But if you want to get ahead, if you are willing to take risks, then be prepared to fall, especially if you intend to be an Extra Mile trekker.

The risk of falling and failing is the price we must pay for progress, and the chance doubles as we traverse the Extra Mile.

Roman Catholics believe that Jesus stumbled and fell on the way to his crucifixion, not once but three times. The three alleged falls are numbered among the Catholic Stations of the Cross. Our Catholic companions find comfort in following the Lord along the Via Dolorosa, the zigzag road that cuts through the heart of Jerusalem, the one that invites us to identify with Jesus. Pilgrims still walk those cobble-stoned streets. In so doing they seek to identify with the original Extra-Miler.

Protestants maintain that there is no biblical record of some of Jesus' falls on the way to the cross. However, few dispute the possibility that a person carrying a heavy crossbeam, especially after being beaten severely, might be inclined to collapse under such a weighty load. It is entirely possible that Jesus fell repeatedly, whether or not the events are a matter of public record.

What is known for sure is that Jesus fell during his dark night of the soul. It's in the biblical account. Jesus fell on his face in prayer on the night when he was betrayed by Judas Iscariot, mere hours before setting out on the winding road to Golgotha.

He had gone, as was his custom, to the Garden of Gethsemane to commune with his Father. On this occasion he was accompanied by most of his disciples – notably Peter, James, and John. But even while surrounded by his followers Jesus felt alone, not for lack of companionship, but because he was on an Extra Mile journey – whereas those who professed their undying loyalty to him were satisfied with a casual single mile jaunt. Jesus had come to the garden to pray, not to play. The disciples were merely out for a laconic stroll.

The text says that he "went a little further" than his band of brothers. Is this not the distinguishing feature of every Extra-Miler, to go a little further? The one who would lead must be out in front of the team; must go farther than the lackadaisical disciples; must earn distinction by reason of the distance walked and the accompanying Extra Mile attitude along the way.

In the Garden Jesus actually collapsed, not once, but three times. He fell down repeatedly, by reason of grief and stress, begging his Father to give him a pass on the suffering that portended his soul's bleakest night. Three times he arose to check on his disciples only to find them sleeping. In their exaggerated dreams they were doubtless going the Extra Mile, when in reality they were at a rest stop along the single mile road. They were not sweating, much less sweating drops of blood, as was their suffering Master only a stone's throw away.

Single-mile people are able to snore through a crisis with aplomb, unmoved by the rigorous demands of responsibility. It matters not that the weight of the world rests heavy on a fellow sojourner's shoulders. One-milers are quite content, like the

Roman soldiers of old, to let someone else carry their load. One-mile people do less and, subsequently, fall down less than Extra-Milers. But neither will they ever know the joy and fulfillment of staggering to their feet again, dusting themselves off, and moving on toward success with renewed vigor. They won't ever know the euphoria of getting back up and continuing their journey, especially when the world has counted them down and out.

Jesus did not have to fall to his knees in the Garden of Gethsemane. He didn't have to fall along the Via Dolorosa either. Yet, if he was to share fully in the human experience he needed to fall. Falling is part and parcel of being flesh and blood. In the movie The Passion of the Christ one of the most touching moments is when Jesus, depicted as a toddler, falls down and starts to cry. His mother, Mary, runs to comfort him. The scene whispers: "He was just like us. He fell, too."

However, he got up, didn't He? Therein lies the secret. Whereas falling down is easy, getting up isn't. Anyone can fall. It is a matter of tripping and allowing gravity to do the rest. The impact of shins and elbows with the ground is then inevitable. But picking one's self up and continuing on even though battered and bruised, is Extra Mile behavior. It is an attitude that defies logic and runs counter to our normal inclination. Yes, Jesus fell – but he stood up again and kept moving forward. He invites us all to do the same.

Jesus was not the only one to fall on the night of his betrayal. Simon Peter, Jesus' main disciple, fell figuratively as well. He had boasted that he would never deny his leader. Others might slip and fall, run and hide, but Peter maintained that he would stand firm in the face of all odds and walk the Extra Mile with his Lord while others might falter. However, before the night was over – before the local rooster crowed three times – he had fallen face-first into the quagmire created by his arrogant pride.

It happened like this: After Jesus' arrest at the Garden of Gethsemane he was taken before a succession of kangaroo courts presided over by prejudiced judges. The courts merely went through the motions of justice. The die had already been cast so to speak, the judgment rendered, and the decision made. All knew that Jesus and anyone foolish enough to defend him would be crucified come daylight.

Facing potential guilt by association, Simon Peter ("The Rock") went the Extra Mile all right – but in the opposite direction. Three times he denied ever having met Jesus, throwing in some colorful curse words to add credence to his protestations. Peter, who had vowed to stand, fell. He fell very badly, indeed.

Meanwhile, Judas Iscariot had also fallen. He had also betrayed his rabbi. Filled with remorse he threw the money gained by his chicanery at the feet of the crooked judges who had paid him to lead them to Jesus. He groaned out a few words of remorse. He confessed that he had favored temporal gain over loyalty and eternal reward. Then, in a final flourish, Judas walked outside the city gates and perished by his own hand.

Peter and Judas both went the wrong way on the Extra Mile road that night. They regressed rather than progressed. So why do we now, after 20 centuries, readily name our boys Peter and rarely even name our dogs Judas? I suspect that it has a great deal to do with the fact that though Simon Peter fell he eventually got up again. Judas didn't. Ultimately, the main difference between the two men who stumbled that Thursday evening was simply this: One fell and got up and the other fell and didn't.

At the end of his days Peter got up, once and for all, and finished the Extra Mile assigned to him. Peter asked the soldiers to crucify him upside down, declaring with his final breath that he was not worthy to be martyred in the same upright position as his master many years before.

Have you fallen? If you have, take a moment to embrace the fact that your tribe is large and covers the span of history. Indeed, we have all stumbled. But those who excel and prevail are among the band of enlightened pilgrims who refuse to stay down when they fall down. If you want to know how it works ask Jesus – or Peter. But don't ask Judas. He doesn't have a clue.

Chapter 22: Extra-Milers Do More Than They Promise

All you need to say is simply 'Yes' or 'No'; anything
beyond this comes from the evil one.
~ Jesus in the Sermon on the Mount

Secret #22

When all is said and done, a lot more is said than done. One milers talk; Extra-Milers walk. One-milers are full of hollow assurances, whereas Extra-Milers back up each and every promise with performance.

You can't talk your way into the Extra Mile Hall of Fame. Inductees are enshrined, not for their powers of elocution, but for the influence and impact of their actions upon others. Follow-through is the coin of their realm. What they agree to do, they accomplish. They may occasionally say "no" and pleasantly surprise by delivering anyway, but they'll almost never say "yes" and fail to complete what they have promised. Their motto is "do or die". They make it a habit to produce more than they say.

Jesus told a story about a man who had two sons. He instructed the first son to go work in his vineyard. But the boy balked. "No, I won't go," he said. So, the father moved on to the second son with the same instructions. This son was respectful and compliant. "I will, sir," he said with enthusiasm and apparent sincerity.

However, as it turned out the son who refused to go ultimately went to work in the vineyard, while the son who said he would go changed his mind and didn't show up as promised. "Which of the two did what his father wanted?" Jesus asked. The correct answer was "the first". Granted, neither son's reply was ideal, but the one who did what he was asked to do, although tardily, was more on point than the big talker. The one who did more than he had promised, even though he had initially declined to participate, was the truly obedient son. In the end, he was the Extra-Miler.

The adage may be hackneyed, but still rings true: "Actions speak louder than words." Here's the take-away from Jesus' parable: Say "no" if you can't (and upgrade it to a "yes" later) or say "yes" if you can and then actually do what you say.

Simply stated: Do what you promise – and more if you can.

One-milers are full of wind and fury, froth and bother. They promise the sun and deliver the moon. In their ranks are tradesmen who don't show up for appointments, salespeople who forget to return calls and businesses that find convenient loopholes in their warranties. One-milers talk a good game but don't execute on the court or the field. All of us have heard one-mile promises:

"The check is in the mail."

"I'll have it in tomorrow morning at the latest."

"Your reservation has been made."

"Don't worry about a thing."

"I give you my solemn word."

"I'll call you back within the hour."

"It's all under control."

In the biblical book of Hebrews 11 we are invited to walk through a promenade lined on either side with displays honoring Old Testament men and women of faith. Some of the honorees had speaking parts during their lifetimes, such as Abraham, Moses, and Joseph. However, most of them – including Abel, Enoch, and Rahab – spoke solely by their actions. Their words weren't recorded for posterity. But then again their words aren't necessary for us to follow their stories. They didn't waste a lot of time talking about their faith walk; they actually paced it out, step-by-step and mile-by-mile. As a result not only did they accomplish what they set out to do, namely to keep the faith, but they also surpassed all expectations. They became role models of valor and daring.

During their hike across the pages of the sacred text most of them lurched off the path a time or two. Abraham told half-truths to save his own skin. Moses let his temper get the best of him. Samson lost both his hair and his strength. David proved himself to be a he-man with a she-weakness. They were a flawed bunch, these dubious heroes. But what made them special was how they ended. They all did more than they said and in the end, though they had spasmodic episodes of failure, they ultimately all finished with a flourish.

Arxegos were pioneers of the faith who backed their words up with accomplishment. They did what they said, they did everything that they said, and they often did more than they had said. Jesus Christ is the ultimate arxegos. Hebrews 12 refers to him as the pioneer (arxegos) of our faith. That term in the original text means "initiator, trailblazer, paradigm maker". In ancient times an arxegos was a valiant soldier who had done remarkable exploits. Such a champion did his "talking" on the battlefield, not in the barracks. To become an arxegos required a soldier to do something no one else had ever done in combat before, usually eventuating in the dispatch of one's enemy with the enemy's very own weapons.

In the Old Testament, David's "mighty men" were all pioneers. For example, Benaiah attacked a seven-and-a-half foot Egyptian with a club, took his spear away from him, and then killed him with it. Eleazar single-handedly defended a field, fending off a host of Philistines in the process, fighting until his hand became so cramped that he couldn't release his grip to let go of his sword at sunset.

In a well-made action movie you should be able to mute the sound and follow the story line fairly well by just watching the action on the screen. You will soon figure out who the good guys and the bad people are by observing their behavior. The protagonists and antagonists will become apparent without a lot of dialogue. The heroes and the villains may be equally well dressed and good-looking, but what they are thinking behind their chiseled features and tailor-made suits will become manifest via their actions soon enough. They may look alike, but they don't act alike.

Even so, there is a significant difference between the promises made by one-milers and Extra-Milers. The former depend on words and dialogue to tell their story. The latter rely on actions and performance to build their reputation. The Bible lauds the one who "makes a promise to his own hurt and does not change".

The Extra-Miler keeps his or her word, even when it is inconvenient. They both promise and deliver.

Recently I was in the market for a car. I searched the Internet and found the exact vehicle I wanted at a dealership a hundred miles away. We made a deal. They would hold the car for me until Thursday. I would come over on that day for a test drive and, all things being equal, would then buy the car. I was given assurances that they would hold the car until I arrived.

On Wednesday I called to make sure that the car would be ready for me on the next day, only to be told that they had just sold it. Now, I understand that "a bird in the hand is worth two in the bush", but to me a promise is a promise. Our agreement had been violated and I was left disappointed, though not disillusioned. I had been the subject of one mile, shortsighted business ethics – standard procedure in all too many establishments. I reasoned that it has happened before and will happen again. Move on.

So I went back to the computer and, after a lengthy search, found an even nicer version of the car at a dealership in Florida, 1300 miles from my home near Boston. Once again I was promised that the car would be held for me. Should I believe them? I was going down to Florida anyway, so I decided to try again. I had little to lose.

As it turned out the Florida store did far more than they promised. A salesman picked me up at the airport, drove me 30 miles to the dealership, put me behind the wheel of the car that looked exactly as pictured in the ad, tweaked a couple of things that needed calibration, and treated me to sweet Cuban coffee as I signed the paperwork. The sales team and I became friends. I drove the car for a week and then took the car back to them so that it could be put on a transporter to be shipped home. We had some more coffee and the same salesman whisked me back to the airport. He refused the generous tip that I offered him explaining, "I'm just happy to serve you." As I said, they did far more than they promised, unlike the dealership a mere hundred miles from my New England home.

Would I go back to Florida to buy another car at that dealership? Yes, in a heartbeat. I have already referred two southern customers to them, with more to come.

I wrote the CEO of that chain of dealerships commending his staff and urging that all of them get raises. I have used this story before audiences on more than one occasion, to illustrate how keeping one's word and doing more than promised can bring long-term gains. The nearby dealership sold only one car the day they broke their promise to me. The Florida dealership is still harvesting the benefits of a single promise – made, kept, and even exceeded. If I have my way they will sell many cars because they kept their word to me and outperformed all expectations.

The first mile is the wide road on which promises are made. The Extra Mile is the narrow road on which promises are fulfilled and exceeded. Say yes or say no, but whatever you say, deliver on your promise. The cost of talk is cheap, but the cost of breaking a promise is steep.

Let's keep our word, lest our word keep us from the laurels of Extra Mile success.

Chapter 23: Extra-Milers Understand and Manage Speed Wisely

"One day Peter and John were going up to the
temple at the time of prayer..."
~ Acts 3:1

Secret #23

Recently a friend of mine brought some merchandise up to the checkout counter at a local department store. The two young ladies behind the counter were obviously bored and didn't care who knew it. They didn't appear to see him, a long-time customer, even though he was standing a mere three feet away from them. Ignoring him they both turned around at the same time, almost as though they had choreographed the move, and glanced at the clock behind them through sleepy eyes. One yawned while the other clicked her gum. "I can't believe it," groaned the gum-snapper between theatrical chomps, "it's only three o'clock!"

When Miss Wrigley Spearmint announced the time, my friend commented that he suddenly felt a sense of alarm and dread. His was an entirely different reaction to hers. "Oh no, I can't believe it," he thought glancing at his watch in hope that the checkout girl was wrong, "it's already three o'clock!"

What was the difference between the two responses? The clock controlled the cashier's day, whereas my friend's day was guided by his destination. Hence, the exclamation "it's three o'clock" meant entirely different things to each of them. The two cashiers merely wanted to "get their shift over with". My friend had clear priorities that depended on accomplishment by sundown, thus his slightly harried response when he realized the lateness of the hour.

One-mile people usually live exclusively by the clock. They are more interested in spending time than in investing it. When it comes to work the goal is merely to put in the hours, collect a check, and enjoy the weekend before starting the endless cycle all over again on Monday morning. If it were possible to do so, many one-milers would fast-forward their life to the day of retirement, forgoing the adventures of the intervening years in favor a short, listless existence on a comfortable sofa at the twilight of life. Hyperbole? Perhaps. But there is a grain of truth in exaggeration.

On the other hand the Extra-Miler owns a watch but doesn't live by it. A clock is a device to measure the interval during which a stated goal is met, and the amount of time expended is secondary to the excellence of the task accomplished. The universal mathematical formula is that distance divided by speed equals time. (For example, if I'm traveling 500 miles at 50 miles-per-hour it will take me 10 hours to make the journey.) But which of the variables is most important to the traveler: Covering the distance as quickly as possible – or enjoying the scenery while taking leisurely back roads?

That depends on the traveler's objective. If a loved one has taken ill and the goal is to get to the hospital quickly, then speed is of the essence. The 500 miles may need to be covered in seven hours or so. But if a couple is on their honeymoon, then velocity will quietly give way to the leisure of winding byroads. In that case a 500-mile journey may take upwards of a week. How fast we travel versus how far we go can only be determined by the stated purpose of the trip.

Isn't it remarkable that we have no record of Jesus ever running? Of course, that doesn't mean that he never ran, but it does suggest that his normal pace was probably deliberate rather than rapid. When his dear friend Lazarus was very sick Jesus' speed was measured, even during such a significant crisis. He knew where he was going and he knew how long it would take him. He knew what he would do when he arrived. His purpose and his pace were intertwined.

Jesus was habitually traversing the Extra Mile – and he understood that the Extra Mile usually takes longer than the first one. He knew that rushed ministry runs the risk of trading quantity of time for quality of ministry. He knew that unnecessarily rapid service doesn't usually serve anyone effectively. So, Jesus' speed tended to match the importance of his mission. Indeed, it seems that the more important the journey, the more purposeful became his step. However, Jesus never meandered. He always had a specific destination even when his cadence was moderate.

I serve in occupational ministry. I try to listen patiently to every need and look distraught people in the eye when they come in for counseling appointments. However, I must confess to fidgeting mentally more often than I'd like to admit. By nature I am not a patient person. I prefer to get to the bottom line quickly. I like reports that are only one page in length. I struggle with details and committee meetings. Speed has been part of my nature from the time I was propelled from the womb onto this unsuspecting planet. However, I'm not defending my proclivity for swift accomplishment as a noble thing. Indeed, at this point in life I am inclined to feel that it is not. I have come to believe that hurry is not merely of the devil, but it is actually his most pronounced personification.

So, to decide how fast we should travel along the Extra Mile requires that we first determine our purpose. What is our goal? In Roman times the goal of the first mile was simply to get it done. The inconvenienced Jewish merchant who had been commandeered to carry to pack of a sneering soldier didn't want to dawdle. His only objective was to plop the enemy's knapsack down at the next mile marker so that he could be on his way. Perfunctory accomplishment was the part of the formula that appealed to the Israelite who had been dragged away from his personal agenda to be pack animal to a hated Roman warrior.

However, the Extra Mile was a matter of both distance and opportunity to the one who had made a deliberate choice to go the greater distance. No longer was the incentive to merely get the onerous task done and over with. The intention was to reverse the tables; the unwilling to become the willing; the one aggrieved to become the forgiving servant.

That's the way of the Extra Mile.

It is always three o'clock for someone, and not just at the local department store's checkout counter. One-milers everywhere sigh at the prospect of the slow passage of time with too little to do. However, if we aren't careful, even devoted Extra-Milers may miss an opportunity to serve at the three o'clock hour. When we get too preoccupied with speed over purpose, we may end up no better than a one-miler, perhaps just a bit faster.

On the night before his crucifixion Jesus prayed to his Heavenly Father: "I have finished the work that you gave me to do." How could he say that he had completed God's work when there still were so many sick people that he hadn't healed? Did he not see them? Had he grown weary of the very Extra Mile that he championed so passionately?

Two years later Peter and John were going to the Temple to pray. In so doing they went through a gate they had entered a hundred times before, often in the company of Jesus. That day, in their haste to make it to the prayer gathering on time, they almost walked past a crippled man who was begging at the gate. They had rushed by him scores of times over many years on their way to ask God to give them an opportunity to serve their community. They had never really noticed the man and the need because they were always focused on speed over purpose.

But on that day they slowed down, stopped, and actually looked at the beggar who sat holding the beat up cup in his calloused hand. In turn he looked at them. Suddenly, getting to the prayer meeting punctually took a backseat to serving this poor man whose legs had been shriveled from birth. They offered him help and hope. Soon the lame man was dancing, and in a manner of speaking so were Peter and John. They had renewed their devotion to the Extra Mile and more importantly, to their Master who had taught them to walk it with such focus and deliberation.

So, let's all manage our speed wisely lest we sprint where we should walk and, in so doing, run past a golden opportunity to serve. Let's look every customer in the eye and actually listen to him or her. Let's get down on eye-level with our younger sons and daughters and take time to pay attention to their story. Let's not be so consumed by what is on our own agenda that we forget the agenda of those we have been called to serve.

It is three o'clock to someone, somewhere. At least for today let's covenant to understand and manage our speed wisely. Let's walk together slowly, fellow pilgrims. Who knows what we will see, who we will meet, and what we may be called upon to do.

Chapter 24: Extra-Milers Head in the Right Direction

"There is a way that appears to be right, but in the
end it leads to death."
~ Proverbs 14:12

Secret #24

One day, back when I lived in Chicago, I was driving on the Edens Expressway to an appointment in the northern suburbs. Over the previous weeks I had slowly slipped into the bad habit of not allowing myself enough time to get to meetings unhurried and unharried. It seemed that I was perpetually racing to make up for minutes that I had lost here and there by reason of poor time management choices. The upshot was that I often felt internally frazzled when I finally got to my destination and as a result I wasn't always focused the way I wanted to be when making a presentation or participating in a board meeting.

However, on that day I was rather pleased with myself. Not only was I on schedule for a change, but also I actually had time to spare. Furthermore, I was multi-tasking as I drove with the flow of traffic to my appointment. I quietly congratulated myself on being a model of efficiency. I estimated that I would arrive well before the hour of my speaking engagement allowing me to get everything set up and have ample time to gather my thoughts. I might even have a quiet moment to grab a cup of java and a bagel beforehand.

It was then that I saw a road sign that threw all of my lofty projections out the window. The good news was that I was making excellent time. The bad news was that I was going in the wrong direction! I was heading south instead of north.

To this day I don't know how I did it, but while getting off one ramp and onto another I must have somehow reversed my direction. Consequently, instead of being on schedule I was actually way behind. Instead of getting closer to my goal I was moving away from it. Yes, I was most certainly going the Extra Mile – but I was going the Extra Mile in the wrong direction.

All I could think of at that moment was the cryptic dialogue between Alice and the Cheshire Cat in Alice in Wonderland:

[Alice:] "Would you tell me, please, which way I ought to go from here?"

"That depends a good deal on where you want to get to," said the Cat.

"I don't much care where..." said Alice.

"Then it doesn't matter which way you go," said the Cat.

"...so long as I get somewhere," Alice added as an explanation.

"Oh, you're sure to do that," said the Cat, "if you only walk long enough."

It is entirely possible to be both an Extra-Miler and also be headed in the wrong direction. The two aren't mutually exclusive. In fact, Extra-Milers probably have a greater propensity for going the wrong way than one-milers. Why? Mathematically we double our chances of becoming misdirected or confused when traveling two miles as opposed to just one.

Along with the turbo-charged Extra Mile desire to serve may come an unwillingness to listen to the one we are trying to assist. We begin to make assumptions about the soldier whose pack we are shouldering, about what he or she wants. He may need to go to Jericho, but we incorrectly presume that the destination is Joppa. In such cases our best efforts to help someone actually end up hurting them.

One Christmas the members of our church board wanted to do something special for all of the widows. They wished to give them nice gifts and for the whole experience to be a big, pleasant surprise. So in making their decision they applied the Golden Rule: "Do unto others as you would have done unto you."

Using that rubric they concluded that boxes of chocolate candy would be in order. (After all, who doesn't like candy?) As a result they bought the very finest chocolate, enlisted help to wrap the boxes in beautiful paper, and distributed them to all of the older ladies in the church. The widows seemed appreciative, but later admitted that more than a few of them were diabetics or on diets that disallowed chocolate candy.

Not to be deterred, the deacons decided to make amends by getting the women the best hams money could buy for Easter. Later they found out that most of the ladies went to the homes of relatives for Easter dinner, and that their refrigerators were so small they couldn't cram the hams into their tiny freezers. Once again, a blessing had become a burden. The intrepid Extra Mile deacons had second-guessed wrongly, yet again, and the result was an Extra Mile hike in the wrong direction.

The widows took the church leaders' attempts at bringing the element of surprise into their holidays with aplomb, even good humor. In fact, they thought their misdirected efforts to be sweet, kind, and thoughtful. By this time the process was becoming rather funny and everyone in the church was kidding the deacons, who took it all good-naturedly. However, the next time they got gifts for the widows they asked them beforehand what they wanted. The answer came back loud and clear: Gift certificates, the very thing the men had been trying to avoid in their sincere desire to please!

Many an Extra-Miler has gone the commendable second mile, but the wrong way. We do it by misreading love languages. We assume. We project. We make decisions based upon our personal preferences rather than those of the people we most want to help. For example: Husbands go the Extra Mile in the wrong direction when they give their wives toasters or vacuum cleaners as anniversary gifts.

Bosses go the Extra Mile in the wrong direction when they give employees bonuses when their workers would prefer more time off.

Clerks go the Extra Mile in the wrong direction when they diligently restock the shelves while customers wait impatiently at the cash register.

Speakers go the Extra Mile in the wrong direction when they address questions that no one in the audience is asking.

Servers go the Extra Mile in the wrong direction when they work intently on getting the bill added up correctly and quickly, even though what we really want is more coffee.

Marriages dissolve, politicians are voted out of office, customers walk out the door vowing never to return, and teens feel that their parents do not love them, all because of misunderstandings surrounding this basic precept – namely, that the Extra Mile must be traveled in the direction of the one we are trying to please for it to be truly effective. Our spouse, our neighbor, our employer, our child, our friend, our fiancé is the person who should be dictating the direction of the Extra Mile, not us. The servant doesn't hold the compass; the one being served holds it. The centurion has the final word.

Our family used to go to a charming little French bistro that had great food, a lovely atmosphere, and subdued complimentary décor. The place was a gem. The only problem was the main waiter. He gave the impression that he knew the food selection that was best for each diner who entered "his" restaurant. The man fancied himself a connoisseur, not only of continental cuisine, but also of what constituted a healthy diet for each and every person seated around one of "his" tables.

The fellow meant well. In his own way he was diligent and attentive. He was an Extra-Miler in one sense, but let's just say that he too often went in the wrong direction.

For example, if the Charles de Gaulle-like waiter felt you were lacking in iron in your diet, he ordered liver and onions on your behalf, even if you asked for salmon. If he concluded that you were a bit overweight, you would get no ice cream for dessert, no matter how much you cajoled him. Your wish was most certainly not his command. He was going to serve you the way he thought you should be served, not the way you wished to be served.

At first it was humorous to us. It was like going to an old roadside diner with Suzy the waitress in a hairnet, calling you "honey" while snapping her gum and taking your order. Then it became annoying. Finally we stopped going to that otherwise-charming little place altogether. It was sad. The waiter, for all of his snootiness, meant well. But he was going the wrong way and no amount of persuasion could get him headed on the Extra Mile path preferred by those he was supposed to serve.

Every now and then we read of a football player who gets disoriented and unwittingly runs the wrong way, toward the opponent's goal posts. Or an airline pilot lands his commercial jet at the wrong airport. Or a commencement speaker gets the name of the college mixed up with another institution with a similar name. The football player, the pilot, and the speaker are all well-meaning professionals – but they are also, however innocently, headed in the wrong direction.

Long ago a sage by the name of Solomon said that there is a way that seems right to the traveler but it ends badly. When we are no longer truly serving those whose bags we are carrying, when we are on a tangent rather than the main path, our Extra Mile mission is seriously compromised. It is then time to ask questions rather than make assertions. At that juncture we should go back to the one-mile marker and start afresh on our Extra Mile journey.

We should check to ensure that we are following in the footsteps of the Rabbi who asked of sick and needy people, "What do you want me to do for you?" Only then, after listening to their reply did Jesus act. He never went in the wrong direction, not once. He didn't foist his agenda on others, even when he knew it was in their best interest.

The good news is that on the day I referenced at the start of this chapter I was able to get off of the expressway, loop back around, and get on track again without too much trouble or delay. A valuable lesson was learned at the expense of relatively little harm. I discovered that two miles in the wrong direction isn't the same as Extra Mile behavior. However, neither is stubbornly continuing on the wrong course because admitting the mistake would be too costly.

The integrity of the path we are traveling is worth the effort it will take to turn around. There will be plenty of time to go the Extra Mile when you and I are once again headed in the right direction. But until we get reoriented our best efforts will prove useless, and even counter-productive.

So, let's do a U-turn. Let's buy the right gift, serve the requested food, listen to our team, speak words that strengthen, and land the plane at the airport printed on the passengers' tickets. Anything less is really one-mile behavior times two or, in extreme cases, one-mile behavior minus two. Thus, as soon as we've checked our direction, let's pick up the pack of the person we're serving and hike with them. Ask the person with the map and the compass where they want to go, then cheerfully help them to get there.

One of the best questions we can ask in any relationship is: "What will make you happy?" You and I can have the box of chocolates we like so much when it is our turn to be served, but for now – let's think gift certificates if that's what the widows want. Let's think a day at the spa if that is what our wife wants. Let's deliver pizza rather than escargot if that's what the customer has ordered. Going beyond the call of duty is good and going the Extra Mile is desirable, as long as it doesn't try to take the one we are serving in the wrong direction. Then it becomes a bother rather than a blessing.

On the Extra Mile road it isn't about us. It's about the person we are serving. Two miles – in the right direction – is the way to go for all concerned.

Chapter 25: Extra-Milers Accept Both Themselves and Others

"Whoever welcomes one of these little children in my
name welcomes me..."
~ Mark 9: 37

Secret #25

I have performed quite a few weddings. The marriage vows are normally exchanged at a church altar. During the ceremony I usually take a moment to suggest that the bride and groom should take care to not try to turn the word "altar" into "alter". I share with them that such attempts are usually futile and frustrating. Indeed, those who insist on misspelling and interchanging the two words, altar and alter, frequently end up in a counselor's office within a year or so. Why?

Altar and alter – the first is a noun; the second is a verb. One is a place of personal sacrifice; the other is an attempt to modify someone or something. An altar is where we transform ourselves for the sake of others; to alter is an attempt to change others for our personal benefit. An altar is a selfless place, whereas to alter can become a selfish act. The two words are miles apart.

Trouble is often discernable during premarital sessions. At an early meeting the bride-to-be may let out a laugh, one that is more of a snort than a giggle, after which the future groom rolls his eyes as if to say, "I will alter that embarrassing chortle once we're married." Really? Later on she watches with restrained irritation as her husband-to-be drums his fingers on the table. Her sigh and thinly disguised body language say, "That bad habit is going to stop – right after the honeymoon!" Seriously?

Those who study marriages have found that couples who have learned how to accept each other's uniqueness and foibles tend to stay together and be much happier than those who persist in trying to alter one another. No one wants to be someone's project. We long to be embraced for who we are, not for whom we can be or may be after we become neater or more debonair. When a person gets the idea that he or she will only truly be loved, accepted, and forgiven when a certain standard has been met, inevitable resistance sets in. Anger and resentment quickly follow. At this juncture "over my dead body" becomes the battle cry. The strange laugh and the finger drumming will most likely continue as a sign of control by the perpetrators, even after the alleged wrongdoer is convinced that it is in his or her best interest to change.

Extra-Milers tend to have a "do or die", "no pain no gain", "you snooze you lose" mindset. There is certainly nothing wrong with setting high standards for one's self and wanting to go over and beyond in life. Where such a philosophy becomes problematic is when we haven't been given permission to be change agents by the ones we are trying to transform. We have every right to change ourselves, but until those we are trying to improve have granted carte blanche to us to do the same for them, we should not presume to transform our fellow hikers. As the old saying goes: "A man convinced against his will is of the same opinion still." The proverb most certainly applies to women as well.

Seldom will "centurions" ask for our company on the first mile for the sake of personal transformation. The initial call to shoulder his backpack isn't to hear our catchy aphorisms, our brilliant tips for success, or revel in our scintillating advice. The centurion merely wants to get from point A to point B, and requires our assistance to do so. The soldier wants help, not coaching or correction. A job must be accomplished; a goal met; a ribbon of pathway traversed. That's it.

There's nothing spectacular about being called upon to carry someone's backpack for the first lackluster mile. Indeed, if any transformation takes place, it is usually in the heart and mind of the one doing the heavy lifting, not within the mind of the demanding centurion.

Then we enter the realm of the Extra Mile. We have done our duty and now we are on overtime. Perhaps we feel that our recent magnanimity gives us permission to point out the defects that need correction in our walking companions. We have been silent and humble throughout the first mile, but as we enter the Extra Mile we will, we feel that we must, speak out. The chortling must stop, now! The finger drumming must cease, today! There is a better way and we truly believe that if those in our company will merely follow our example all will be well with the world.

Needless to say, this rather arrogant attitude seldom has the desired outcome. We have become like a neighbor who comes over to help clean up the kitchen after a cookout, and ends up rearranging all of the furniture throughout the house before leaving. In such an instance helping to wash the dirty dishes is a good thing, admirable Extra Mile behavior for sure. However, rearranging the furniture is exercising an unacceptable level of control that is more like taking a self-centered stroll than going the unselfish Extra Mile.

When Jesus said that we should welcome and accept little children on his behalf he didn't mean that they should be allowed to create a ruckus, disobey, be destructive, or throw tantrums. Clearly some forms of behavior are out of bounds under any circumstances. Acceptance in this context means to embrace toddlers for their uniqueness and differences, not for their childishness.

An ancient proverb tells parents to "train a child in the way he or she should go". It means that fathers and mothers are to find the natural inclination inherent in their children and gently move them in that direction. Some boys are cut out for football and some for poetry. Some girls are predisposed to become CEOs and others to be teachers, musicians, or stay-at-home mothers. More harm than good takes place when parents try to relive their lives through their children.

When most people see a young child their first thought isn't "she needs to sit up straighter", but "she has a lovely smile". For some reason, as we get older we accept children in ways that we do not accept one another upon achieving adulthood. Perhaps we think that older people should instinctively know better. After a certain age, to remark that an acquaintance needs to "grow up" is seldom viewed as a compliment. So we are prone to target people as projects intended for our transformation, rather than works of art calling for our celebration. The goal can too easily become changing everyone, even God, into our own rather limited image. Let's be clear here: This isn't part of the Extra Mile credo.

The only person we have the right to change is our own self, and sometimes we shouldn't even attempt to change ourselves too much. For example, there are actors who, having not been satisfied with their looks, have gone through endless facelifts and other cosmetic surgery. The net result is oftentimes both sad and hideous. They should have left well enough alone. There is a watershed moment when more self-improvement becomes counterproductive.

So, accept the wrinkles. They aren't imperfections; they are medals. Your accent is fine, even endearing. Your smile doesn't need to be that of someone else. By the same token, let's cut some slack to those who travel with us. Everyone needs a break from the addiction of constant transformation.

Of course, if we are behaving immorally, unethically, or illegally, we should change. Sin and selfishness aren't part of acceptance theory. Child-likeness is commendable; childishness is not. The former is a virtue; the latter is a vice. Perhaps the best precept concerning acceptance is a quote oft attributed to Augustine: "In essentials, unity; in non-essentials, liberty; in all things, charity."

My wife and I recently did a mini-triathlon together. She had competed the previous year and done well. Her enthusiasm led me to believe that I should join her. Although the race proved grueling, we had a lot of fun both in preparation for and execution of the event. What made it particularly enjoyable is that we accepted each other's strengths and weaknesses. She did some things better than I did and vice versa. Rather than criticize each other's running, kayaking, or biking styles we tried to encourage each other. The end result was that we complemented rather than competed. Together we accomplished much more than had we tried to go it alone – and we covered much more than a mere Extra Mile in so doing.

Let's ask one another: What would the Extra Mile pilgrimage look like if we tried valiantly to accept ourselves and others the way we accept little children? Would our marriage improve? Would our relationship with employees, colleagues, and coworkers get a booster shot? Would we get along better with our teenage children? Would our friendships become even tighter? Would our church become a place where talents and abilities were a showcase for collective grace rather than self-aggrandizement and criticism? Would the factions and parties within our country be less at odds?

Jesus felt loved and accepted when visiting the home of his friends, Mary and Martha. Mary usually listened to him, whereas

Martha cooked for him. Once Martha became indignant with Mary because she wasn't helping with the meal she was cooking for Jesus. She angrily complained to the Lord, who diplomatically patched things up between the two sisters. In essence the Master said, "Ladies, why don't you accept each other instead of fighting? Martha, you serve; Mary, you sit. Accept your different ways of expressing your love for me. After all it's supposed to be for me, not you, right?"

There is a legend that tells of another meal Martha fixed for Jesus a few weeks after the first one. Jesus had agreed to come by at a certain time for supper. As usual Martha was scurrying around, a bit harried and frustrated. To make matters worse, in the midst of her preparations a little boy knocked on her door and asked for some bread. She sent him off with the curt admonition: "Don't bother me now, child. I'm getting ready for Jesus, the great teacher, who is coming to my house for supper. Come back tomorrow."

Then a young girl called through the window to her. Could she ask Mary to read her a story? Again, Martha responded with impatience. "Not now. I'm too busy. Later."

Right on time the supper was ready. But where was Jesus? A film began to settle on the gravy and the falafels started to get cold. Martha was upset with Jesus. She was hurt, indignant, and on the verge of tears. When Jesus arrived, a half hour late, she barked at him, "Master, where have you been? I have been waiting for you! The food is getting cold." In the legend Jesus is said to have replied, "Martha, I already came to your house twice. I was the little boy; I was the tiny girl. You didn't recognize me in disguise, and because you didn't recognize me you wouldn't let me in."

While trudging the Extra Mile the billowing dust may blind us momentarily to the reality of who is really in our motley band. Jesus may be the rough centurion. He may be the leper. He may be our spouse. He most certainly is the child. "Whoever welcomes one of these little children in my name welcomes me..."

Finally, I realize that putting the word "themselves" before "others" in the title of this chapter isn't the best grammar. However, I submit that it is procedurally correct. For it is only when we accept the unique walking style given to us by our Creator that we can and will embrace the way our fellow pilgrims stride. His or her pacing may be quite different from ours, but that's acceptable among Extra Mile hikers. The main thing isn't the form, but the function – and the function is to go the Extra Mile, together, in harmony, celebrating our uniqueness to the glory of the God who made us all.

Chapter 26: Extra-Milers Admit Errors Quickly

"First go and be reconciled ... then come and offer
your gift."
~ Jesus in the Sermon on the Mount

Secret #26

It is easy to err, but rather hard to admit an error. When we make a mistake our natural fallback position is denial. Problem, we ask, what problem? Even when the evidence is incontrovertible, with the proof of the blunder peeping out from under the blankets of our indignant protests, we tend to continue to maintain our innocence. Why is that? Why do we find it so difficult to simply acknowledge our wrong? Why do we take uneasy solace in a lie, when the truth can set us free?

In the Bible sin means "to miss the target". Sometimes the miss is deliberate, but more often than not it is just a well-intentioned miscalculation. To err is human. We aim to hit the bull's-eye, but we hit a bystander instead. We try to do something good and it turns out badly. The compliment gets mangled and we insult rather than encourage. An action or gift comes too late or is misunderstood. Our motives are questioned, our character impugned. Can we do nothing right? So, we do what seems to be the next best thing. We deny complicity, hunker down, and hope that the storm will soon pass by.

It seldom does. Our spouse makes it clear that our silence or absence isn't the response he or she was looking for. The voters want to know why the candidate made such a bizarre, ill-timed statement. The environmentalists aren't content with the reason given at the press conference for the huge oil spill. Shareholders, parishioners, neighbors, students, allies, and friends all suspect that the excuse being proffered is considerably off the mark. They are all wondering why we are digging in when we should be fessing up. Indeed, why aren't we?

The reasons are legion: Pride. Shame. Potential lawsuits. Anger. Fear. Loss of status. Hatred. Hubris. Lack of self-esteem. Weariness. Cynicism. Character. Disconnectedness. Vanity. Deception. The list goes on and is very long, indeed. Add to it if you wish.

By contrast, Jesus said that if a person is on his or her way to worship and remembers an unaddressed misunderstanding with another person, the issue should be solved before the sacrifice is offered. One shouldn't ignore a broken relationship until it becomes toxic and irreparable. Fix the problem first. Admit the error quickly. Don't allow for the cement of opinions and attitudes to harden overnight. Say the three phrases that tend to mend: I'm sorry, it was my fault, and please forgive me. Ask three questions: How can I make this right? What would make you happy? What would it take to win your trust again?

One-milers shift blame or point the finger. The same workers who don't say "thank you" when you make a purchase tend not to say "I'm sorry" when you are forced to make a return due to their clerical error. We've all met members of these large fraternities and sororities of one-mile people. This person is in customer service – but shouldn't be. That person is in management – but won't be for long. They are in politics – but probably not after the next election.

Extra-Milers, on the other hand, admit their errors without undue arm-twisting or argument. They don't cringe and cower, but neither do they bluster and become intractable. They know the potential danger of winning the battle while losing the war. Is it so difficult to empathize, soothe, and apologize? It shouldn't be. Indeed, such acts of humility most often lead to marital harmony, customer satisfaction, voter loyalty, peace and civility, and trusting relationships.

Several years ago my wife and I decided to try out a new restaurant in our neighborhood. It appeared to be a classy place with a friendly maître d', white linen tablecloths, an extensive wine list, and not your run-of-the-mill food. We went at lunchtime and were immediately seated at a well-lit, comfortable table for two. The server handed us both new leather-bound menus with the promise that she would return momentarily to answer our questions and take our beverage orders.

Five minutes went by. Then ten. We were on a rather tight schedule so I signaled to the maître d'. He quickly came over to our table and politely asked how he could be of service. I replied that our server had not returned for quite a while; that it would be helpful if he could help expedite the process since we had not set aside time for a leisurely lunch. He said that he would check into the matter and get right back to us.

True to his word, in short order he returned. He had a perplexed look on his face. He seemed embarrassed. I could tell that he was having a hard time formulating what he was about to say. With a dazed expression he stammered: "No one knows for sure, but the server apparently went home. She told someone that she couldn't take the pressure of the job anymore. I don't know what to say, sir. We thought we had hired the right people, but apparently something went wrong. I am so sorry. But if you'll allow me, I'll take care of you myself."

We took him up on his offer and he served us very well, indeed. The salad and entrée were delicious. The maître d's warmth and humor soon made us forget the earlier faux pas. The coffee was especially good, and as an added bonus it was served in a unique cup and saucer. When the meal came to an end the maître d' asked if he could do anything else.

"Well," I said hesitantly, "I really like the cup and saucer. If it isn't too much to ask I'd like to buy a set. Is that possible?" He replied: "Let me see what I can do for you, sir."

With that he disappeared into the kitchen and emerged shortly thereafter with a small bag containing the neatly packaged answer to my request. Then I asked for the check. "There is no charge," he said. "And the cup and saucer are a token gift for your kindness in understanding our first week's start-up jitters. Again, I'm sorry. I can only hope you and your wife will come again."

Over the years not only did we return but we also brought scores of guests with us. Every time we introduced new people to what soon became one of our favorite eateries, we'd tell them the story of our first visit. We'd share about how a server's potentially disastrous lapse, when quickly admitted and corrected by the alert management, became a bridge to ultimate success. And, while drinking coffee from the cup given to me by the maître d' many years ago, I will often illustrate to an audience how an error, when owned and acknowledged, can actually end up winning a lifelong loyal customer. Mistakes, when rectified properly and quickly, can lead to a happier ending than had the error not been made in the first place.

However, the mea culpa must have certain key characteristics. Among the foremost of these are humility, compassion, honesty, and forthrightness. Sometimes we may be apologizing for ourselves, one-on-one, but on other occasions we may find ourselves the spokesperson for a company or a group. While there is no need to grovel, the acknowledgment should be sincere. An "I-did-wrong-but-you-did-too" kind of confession will only make matters worse. Here is a seven-word statement that I've found to work most of the time: "I'm sorry. I apologize. Please forgive me." The question "What can I do to make it right?" is usually an effective conclusion to genuine contrition.

People and entities that persist in doing the rope-a-dope routine when it comes to admitting error usually end up with regrets. Examples? The Exxon Valdez. Richard Nixon. British Petroleum. FEMA during Hurricane Katrina. Need I go on?

Years ago I had an associate who got into a verbal jousting match with the secretary of a person with whom he wanted to do business. By my colleague's ready acknowledgment it was a somewhat heated exchange. The conversation didn't end well. However, instead of my associate coming into my office immediately thereafter with remorse, he seemed to revel in his rhetorical triumph over the secretary. He felt that he had set her straight and said that he was going to tell her boss about her attitude toward him when next they met.

Having heard a good part of the conversation through my open office door I knew that there was another side to the story. Yes, the secretary had been abrupt and even rude, but so had my friend. I also knew that the secretary's boss valued her highly and that though she might be reprimanded, in the end my colleague would probably never get the business from that company that he desired. The secretary was the gatekeeper to the sales department and would ultimately have the last word. My associate had won the battle, but he had also lost the war.

As he and I went over what had just occurred, it became increasingly clear to my colleague that by reason of the recent argument he had effectively lost his opportunity to meet with the boss, a man he very much needed to contact. What should he do? I knew the secretary he had offended, so armed with that knowledge I made a suggestion: Go to her office in person and apologize. Take flowers in hand. Be sincere. She was a forgiving person. However, I warned him that if he didn't make it right immediately, well, she was known to bear grudges.

To my friend's credit he recognized that he had reacted disproportionally. Guided by sincere contrition rather than manipulation he went to the secretary's office. At first she was standoffish, but when she discerned that he genuinely meant what he was saying, she relented. She liked the flowers, too. They ended the day well and became good friends thereafter. Oh, and my colleague was able to see the boss who, because of the secretary's glowing recommendation, gave him what he needed and more.

As it turns out, confession and reparation really are good for the soul – and they are good for marriages, businesses, friendships, races, and communities, too. The original Extra-Miler said it best: "First go and be reconciled – then come and offer your gift." Go, then come – and do it without delay. Do it quickly.

Let's not make the customer or neighbor pry an apology out of us. This is one case wherein haste doesn't equal waste. A heart-felt, timely acknowledgment of a wrong, real or perceived, can make the difference between success or failure along the Extra Mile road.

.

Chapter 27: Extra-Milers Live to Serve

"Whoever wants to become great among you must
be your servant..."
~ Jesus in Mark 10:43

Secret #27

We will never know whether or not we have the heart of a servant until someone treats us like one.

There is a significant difference between acting like a servant and actually being a servant. The former is a self-serving skin-deep 9-to-5 charade; the latter is an others-serving heart-felt 24/7 attitude.

A waiter can feign servanthood for an entire shift because he knows that his potential tips depend upon how courteously he serves his customers. He may mutter under his breath to his colleagues in the kitchen about the people at table seven, but he won't dare show his disdain to them directly for obvious reasons. However, once he is off the clock that same waiter may well become demanding and tyrannical towards his family and peers at home. His rationale might be that he has served discourteous diners at work for eight hours, and now others should bow under the yoke of his discourtesy. In his rulebook turnaround is fair play. I ask you: Is this genuine servanthood or a mere facade?

On the other hand consider the retired secretary who now serves as a volunteer at a hospital information booth. For several decades she typed, answered phones, booked airplane tickets, served grouchy clients, fielded tough questions, and put up with a cranky boss. Throughout her storied career she almost always maintained her composure. Now she has moved to warmer climes and has sufficient resources to take it easy. She doesn't need to work any longer. So, why is she looking up the room numbers of sick people and answering the questions of their inquiring loved ones for free? I submit that over the years she has learned this chapter's Extra Mile secret: namely, that success in life is indexed to how well we serve others.

At Christmas we pause to remember someone who had the right to be born a king, but entered his own planet as a pauper. He could have slept his first night in a hand-carved bassinet lined with ermine, but instead started life swaddled in rags and surrounded by barnyard animals. He was entitled to the pomp and circumstance of a palace, but he slipped onto the stage of this life via a backwater village, unheralded and unnoticed.

From time to time his true identity was nearly compromised. At 12 years of age he instinctively knew far more than his older, highly educated teachers. While in his early thirties his name, Yeshua, was synonymous with unexplainable miracles and exceptional teaching. It was reported that he healed the sick, cast out demons, quelled storms, touched lepers, fed multitudes with a small supply of food, and even raised the dead. Who was this man?

However, despite all of his undeniable power and remarkable abilities he never cut in line, and didn't ask for preferential treatment or demand obeisance. In fact, he was clearly bothered when his closest followers started to act entitled. On one such occasion he told them to stop their game of one-upmanship, that there was already enough hubris to go around. They shouldn't behave like everyone else, he said. The world had it all wrong and upside down: They were called to serve, not to be served.

This tidbit didn't sit well with most of the disciples. Some of them were following their rabbi for the same reason that remoras follow a shark; to garner considerable personal benefits in the shadow of a degree of risk. In fact, two of them had asked their mother to intervene on their behalf, hoping to be appointed cabinet officers in Jesus' new post-Roman administration. On hearing of this maternal ploy the other men had become angry, in large part because they hadn't thought of it first. All of their infighting aside, they had consensus about one thing: Servanthood was the breakfast of weaklings. While Jesus was right most of the time, they were in agreement that he was quite wrong on this issue. The Master had finally erred, they thought, though not irretrievably. He should reverse himself, toughen up, and stop being so nice and kind to everyone.

When Jesus started hinting that part of his full-service ministry included death on behalf of needy people, Simon Peter took the Rabbi aside for a reality check. "Come now, Jesus," said

Peter, "you can't possibly mean it. Go out there and tell the other disciples that it isn't so. This shall not happen to you!"

Wrong again, Simon (the name Jesus called his blustering friend when he was way off base). However, Simon wasn't the only apostle to initially fail the servanthood test. James and John were so bothered by what they perceived to be disrespect from a group of Samaritans that they threatened to call down fire from heaven upon them. Jesus quietly informed the two brothers, (nicknamed Sons of Thunder for their hair-trigger tempers) that they needed to retake the helping-hand quiz. Indeed, at one time or other the Rabbi had to correct all of his men for their pomposity, air of privilege, and continual insistence on VIP treatment.

The coup de grâce of their elitism was manifest at their last meal together. It was a Passover dinner. The tradition was that whoever came in last washed the feet of all the others. From the fact that Peter sat across from John, who was next to Jesus, we deduce that this dubious honor fell to Simon that night. But Peter wasn't one to wash feet. He had made it quite clear over the past three years that he considered such a dirty task beneath him, both literally and figuratively. Let someone else do it.

The men at the table would never forget what happened over the next few minutes. Without saying a word Jesus got up, took a basin, filled it with water, rolled up the sleeves of his best robe, tucked the lower folds of the garment into his belt as was the custom of house slaves, and proceeded to wash all of the dusty feet in the room. By the time the Master got to Simon, who was the last in line, the rambunctious disciple was feeling embarrassed. In a last-ditch effort to salvage his pride he protested that he could not and would not allow his leader to wash his feet. It just wasn't right somehow.

However, Jesus informed him that if he didn't allow him to wash his feet he was going to miss something special. To this Peter replied, with his customary flamboyance: "Then give me a bath, Lord!" Jesus must have smiled at this exaggerated remark, while saying: "Don't get so carried away, Simon. You don't need a bath. But you do need to remember what I've done here. In fact, all of you do. If I am the leader and I washed 24 feet, and two of them belonged to someone who will betray me in a few hours, how much more should you serve others?"

Remarkably, there is no record that Jesus got his feet washed that night. There is no indication of reciprocation. If no one washed the Rabbi's feet that night then he went to the cross with dirty feet, a stark reminder that it is possible to serve and not be served, to help and not be helped. Sometimes we serve others and get little back in return. Sometimes we trudge the Extra Mile and receive no plaudits for our best efforts. What goes around doesn't always come around, at least not in this life.

Dwight Moody was one of the most famous preachers in the golden age of great preaching, the 1800s. He often hosted large conferences at his Northfield Schools campuses in north central Massachusetts. Famous religious leaders of the day came from near and far to teach at the school and also to learn from Mr. Moody.

On one occasion a sizeable group of pastors came to a conference from Europe. They were accustomed to the nightly practice of putting their shoes outside of their doors so that they could be collected, polished, and returned by early morning. However, unbeknownst to them, this wasn't an American custom. There were no shoe-polishers on the payroll at the campus.

As Dwight Moody was walking the halls before going to bed the first night, he saw the shoes lined up and, having traveled in Europe, knew what was expected. He suggested to some of the seminary students that it would be thoughtful of them to clean the shoes for the guests. When no one seemed inclined to serve in this matter, Moody quietly collected all of the shoes and proceeded to polish them himself. If a friend who knocked on his door at midnight had not stumbled on the great preacher polishing shoes, no one would have been the wiser. Moody never told anyone what he had done, but his friend told a few others, who then volunteered to take a turn at shoe polishing for the rest of the conference. The guests never knew what had happened or that the greatest preacher of their era had become a shoe-shiner every night of the conference.

Sometime ago I made a trip to Northfield and stood behind Mr. Moody's pulpit. The curator, knowing that I was a clergyman, asked if I wanted to get my picture taken behind the podium. I declined. I didn't tell her, but I felt it would have been almost sacrilegious for me to stand where this humble man had stood in his service to so many.

A stone's throw from his house is his grave on which is engraved this epitaph from the Bible: "He that doeth the will of God abideth forever." Moody started out as a shoe salesman.

Later in life he didn't feel that it was beneath him to be a shoe polisher. No matter how great his fame, D. L. Moody never lost his servant's heart.

Jesus served. Moody served. All Extra-Milers serve.

"How can I serve you?" should be a question we ask often on the two-mile road. For an Extra-Miler, servanthood is not a job, but a lifestyle. On occasion careful observers will pick up on the trait of our servanthood and strive to replicate this oft-neglected value. But even when they don't, we should serve anyway. "Whoever wants to be great must serve."

Want to be great? Serve!

MILE 2

Chapter 28: Extra-Milers Often Work Without Sufficient Reward

When you've done everything expected of you, be
matter-of-fact and say, 'The work is done. What we
were told to do, we did.'
~ Luke 17:10 (The Message)

Secret #28

Jesus once told the story of a servant who came in from the field after a day of hard work. He was tempted to sit down and order others to serve him, but he didn't do so. Why not? Mainly because he was a servant and at least in that era, that's not what servants did. Servants had no union representation, no time off, no worker's laws to protect them, and no OSHA. They labored from dawn until dusk and were glad to get a pittance at the end of the day. There were no chairs for servants and there was no time to sit.

In Jesus' story the servant washed up after working in the fields since sunrise and then proceeded to fix a nice supper for his boss. Afterwards he made coffee, cleared the table, washed all of the dishes, swept the floor, and finally asked: "Sir, is there anything else I can do for you?"

The boss didn't say to him: "Why, thank you, James. That will be all." This wasn't a Hollywood movie. He didn't say, "I'm truly grateful for the delicious lamb kabobs you fixed. You served me well even though I know you are dog-tired. Excellent job, my good fellow! I appreciate you so much. How would you like a nice raise in your pay? No? Well, at least take tomorrow off."

There is little chance that such a dialogue occurred. Instead, the boss probably grunted dismissively, took another sip of wine, and flicked his little finger. The servant knew what that wordless gesture meant: "Okay, James. You can go to bed for a couple of hours if you must, but don't dare be late to work in the morning or I'll dock your pay!"

I hear an anonymous reader muttering, "Jesus must know my boss, too!" Yes, as a matter of fact, he knew bosses back then and he knows them now. Times haven't changed that much.

Acknowledgments for undertakings performed well have forever been in short supply. It has always been easier to hand out assignments rather than to give accolades; to levy blame over praise; to point out the single task done wrong rather than the ten jobs done right.

I have yet to hear an employee remark that his or her boss has ever gone overboard in the praise department. Bosses don't tend to spread the adulation on so thick that their workers cry out in unison, "Stop! Please, stop! We can't take your kindness much longer. Quit pampering us."

Nice thought, but it just doesn't happen, does it?

By the same token, I don't recall a boss telling me that her subordinates have sufficiently appreciated the raises she has meted out or the extras he has done for them. Few leaders get so many notes of thanks that they ask their subordinates to quit writing. Let's face it: There's a dearth of genuine appreciation these days at every level and truth be told, there always has been.

Jesus' story about the bad boss and the abused worker strives to underline anew the principle of the Extra Mile. Granted, the account is rife with hyperbole – exaggeration for the sake of effect. The kind of treatment Jesus described wouldn't be tolerated today and, in fact, I doubt that most servants were regularly treated that harshly even in his era. So, what was his point then and what is his point even now? It's that Extra Mile disciples, while needing affirmation as much as the next person, find their highest reward in doing a job with excellence to the greater glory of God. Who was the servant in the story working for? Not for his boss, but for The Boss. He was serving for a greater bounty than his next paycheck. He was at work for God.

The Apostle Paul said: "Work willingly at whatever you do, as though you were working for the Lord rather than for people" (Colossians 3:23). He advised employers: "And masters, treat your servants considerately. Be fair with them. Don't forget for a minute that you, too, serve a Master — God in heaven" (4:1).

It always comes back to God. He is the keeper of records, the ultimate equalizer. He sees us when we walk the first mile with a foul-tempered centurion, the one who cannot understand why we don't take the bait of his deliberate abuse. God smiles on us when we offer to go the Extra Mile with a confused soldier, when we say to him: "What we were supposed to do, we did, and more; though not for you, but for God."

Many Extra Mile secrets benefit us. If correctly applied they will most often eventuate in earthly success, promotion, and recognition. However, there will be times when we have done our best and barely get a nod, much less an award. Some of life's most noble deeds won't be acknowledged on earth. The irony is that the more neglected our recognition in this life, the more our deeds will be rewarded in the next. Jesus lambasted the religious gurus of his time for seeking acclaim here. Jesus said that they should enjoy their adulation now for there would be very little of it later.

Does that mean we should shun gain or fame? No, for it is by our income and influence that we can help others. It is by the recognition of our good works that God is honored, too. If there were no wealthy, generous Extra-Milers, there would be no way to extend aid to those less fortunate. Jesus didn't say it is wrong to receive. He said it is better to give than to receive. The former is good, but the latter is very good.

Actually, we receive so that we can give – give of our treasure, time, and talent. The moral of the parable supporting this Extra Mile secret is that in the end it isn't about our image, our possessions, our calendar, or our abilities. We are mere stewards, never owners. We are servants at best. We do the bidding of our Creator and are honored when we are selected to distribute his resources by acts of service in his name.

The fact is that when all is said and done, God will always give more through us than he will give to us.

At the turn of the last century Henry Morrison, a long-term missionary to Africa, was returning home after many years of service in Uganda. His health was broken and his bank account was broken, too. He had labored long and hard for the needy people of that country with seldom a word of thanks. He wondered if anything he had done in a half-century of ministry had been of any ultimate use. As the ship approached the dock at New York Harbor, Henry scanned the platform for a familiar face. Had anyone remembered to come and greet him and his wife? As it turned out, apparently not.

Aboard the same ship, in a swank first class compartment, was former President Theodore Roosevelt who was returning from a safari in Africa. Reporters and photographers were crammed around the gangplank hoping to get a quote from or a picture of the man they affectionately called Teddy. He had been big-game hunting for a few months and was rumored to be returning to run for the Presidency again.

Henry Morrison couldn't help but contrast their welcomes. He had faithfully served God in Africa for most of his life, under the harshest of circumstances, with hardly a break. On the other hand the ex-President had shot a few animals and was now about to give a speech to a mob of attentive fans. The old missionary, never one to seek the limelight, felt strangely depressed. He was surprised by the twin sentiments of bitterness and jealousy that he felt, emotions that had seldom surfaced during his long, quiet career as God's humble servant. He felt ashamed of his anger, which he expressed to his wife, who in turn suggested that he pray about it.

So Henry prayed, pouring out his complaint to God between tears of hurt and surges of anger. Thereafter, he would often tell the story about how in his prayer he "informed" God of his feelings of neglect. "God," the old missionary reportedly said, "I have served you long and faithfully. After investing over half my life in your work I'm now coming home in bad health and with no wealth. Granted, the President is an important man. But all he has done is shoot some elephants and zebras. Yet, he is coming home to a hero's welcome. My wife and I have given our lives to serve you among people who seemed not to have cared. And now we have arrived home and there isn't one person on the dock to greet us. It really isn't fair to arrive home to absolutely no appreciation."

According to Mr. Morrison, when he was through with his rant God softly whispered to him, "Henry, I love and appreciate you. I can understand how you feel neglected. However, Henry, the fact is that you are not home yet. When you truly arrive 'home' you will be amply rewarded and recognized. You have my word on it. But as long as you are in this life keep in mind the following, Henry: You aren't home – yet."

Henry never forgot that line: "You aren't home – yet."

Indeed, no Extra-Miler can afford to forget it. We don't arrive home after traversing just one mile. Even when we've gone the grace-based Extra Mile we often won't see any reward. No matter how deferential we are, the centurion may still growl and kick at journey's end. When that happens we should remember the servant who served the ungrateful boss, and Henry Morrison who came to realize that "home" wasn't a dock in New York.

Home is when, having done all that we were created to do, we hear God say, "Well done, my good and faithful servant. Enter into my joy." Lest we forget, it requires many extra miles of effort to qualify for such holy kudos. In the meantime we should matter-of-factly say to God and ourselves, "The work is finished. What we were told to do, we have accomplished."

Meade McGuire summarizes this secret in this poem...

"Father, where shall I work today?"
And my love flowed warm and free.
Then he pointed out a tiny spot
And said, "Tend that for me."
I answered quickly, "Oh no, not that!
Why, no one would ever see,
No matter how well my work was done.
Not that little place for me."
And the word he spoke, it was not stern;
"Art thou working for them or for me?
Nazareth was a little place,
And so was Galilee."

MILE 2

Chapter 29: Extra-Milers Straighten Paths for Those Yet To Come

"Every valley shall be filled in, every mountain and
hill made low. The crooked roads shall become
straight, the rough ways smooth."
~ Luke 3:5

Secret #29

One of the main roads into the city where I live is very bad,
indeed. It features potholes of such size and depth that I find it
increasingly necessary to get all-too-frequent front-end
alignments for my car. Residents have often asked for the road to
be fixed. Rumor has it that a complete resurfacing project is
planned for the springtime. This news is being met with
furrowed brows because similar promises have been made for
several years in a row, with no accompanying positive outcome.

I have often remarked that what we need to do to get the
road repaired in short order is to invite the President of the
United States to visit our fair city. Since the POTUS would most

likely enter our town by way of the bumpy road, it would undoubtedly require immediate repair lest we all be embarrassed. No one would want the president's limousine to break an axle or burst a tire on the street in question for the entire world to see.

In ancient times a major thoroughfare called The King's Highway ran through the heart of Israel, south to Egypt and north to Syria. If a ruler or potentate wanted to visit one of his dominions he would usually take this road. However, when the king was not planning to use it the highway tended to fall into disrepair. Holes and divots appeared in the road and made travel difficult. The highway became a byway, and zigzagged erratically as travelers invented shortcuts and created tangents of their own. Quite often it was a mess; that is until a ruler decided to use it for a state visit, which then mandated road crews to straighten the crooked parts, fill in the holes, raze the hillocks, and smooth out the rough spots.

Sometimes it isn't enough to walk an Extra Mile. Sometimes we must pause to straighten out the road that has become crooked due to neglect, abuse, or insufficient use. To personally walk the Extra Mile is good, but to fix the road that future pilgrims will eventually hike is equally necessary. Ultimately, the latter has a far greater impact and an even more lasting value than the former.

For example, most parents frequently go the Extra Mile for their children. Raising kids is both a significant challenge and a big sacrifice. Many of us could have had a summer home, a boat, and a couple of sports cars. Instead we made the choice to have a large family. With the passage of time we look back on photo albums full of yellowing snap-shots and wonder if, given the chance, we would go back in time and exchange our costly brood for a chalet, the occasional luxury trip, and more frequent fine dining. I have met very few parents who would give up their offspring for any reason, not even a better lifestyle. Fathers and mothers are usually card-carrying Extra-Milers of the first order.

My wife and I had our first child, Tamara, while we were still in college. Needless to say, money was tight. One Saturday afternoon I was sitting outside in front of our apartment with Tamara when an older man walked up to where I was playing with her. He looked down at the two of us and asked me, "Is that your daughter?" I responded affirmatively. "Would you give her up for a million dollars?" he responded. Unsure of where he was going with this line of questioning I uttered a forceful "No!"

To my single word reply, he smiled and said, "Well young man, then you're a millionaire, aren't you?"

I had never thought of it that way. If I have something that I value at over a million dollars, whatever anyone else may think, I am by definition a millionaire. His perspective helped me then, and continued to help me over the years as we raised several million-dollar kids.

However, as much as we may invest in the here and now, at some point we must pause to ask ourselves what kind of world we are leaving to the next generation. Is their future roadway going to be nicely paved, still under construction, or filled with ruts and potholes? It is admirable to spend our time and resources on feeding, clothing, and protecting our children today. Such an investment calls for unselfish commitment. But what of the ribbon of highway that disappears over the horizon into a future that doesn't include us any longer? When we can no longer hike the Extra Mile road with them, will there be a suitable road left for them to hike at all?

Certainly the part of the Extra Mile road that is devoted to our children and grandchildren is constantly in need of repair and straightening. Hopefully, we are addressing the present demands for the generations to come. However, how about the condition of marriages, friendships, places of employment, and government? What of our community, country, and houses of worship? Will the next generation find that we have been faithful in our stewardship of laws, morals, choices, and ethics? We don't want those who follow to say of us: "They walked their own Extra Mile well enough, but left it littered and pock-marked for our generation."

Hezekiah of Judah was a noble and upright king. He was an Extra-mile ruler. However, on one occasion he made the mistake of showing his treasury to a snooping group of Babylonian envoys. Afterwards a prophet said to Hezekiah: "You shouldn't have done that. The Babylonians will return one day to pillage your storehouses and take many of your subjects away into captivity." Upon hearing this Hezekiah was worried and inquired about the timetable of the prophesied destruction. "In your son's generation – after you're dead and gone," replied the prophet. "Whew!" said Hezekiah, "I thought that the doom and gloom you were talking about was going to come upon me right now. As long as it holds off until after I'm off the scene, that's all right by me. Let God do whatever he wants when I'm gone!"

Alas, there are all too many Hezekiah-like hikers around these days. Such pilgrims are fully invested in going over and beyond in this generation, but haven't made sufficient provision for those who are yet to set foot upon the Extra Mile road. The economy? Social security benefits? The ozone layer? Pollution? Wills and trusts? Education? Morals? Why be concerned about the future? As long as we take care of the road that lies at our feet we are doing all that anyone can expect of us. Right?

Wrong. The Romans were master road builders. They didn't make their routes and vias to merely last a generation. In fact, some Roman roads are still in use today. If a generation is between 20 and 25 years long, then 80 to 100 generations have used many of those ancient roads. Yet, even though they were made to last, repairs have been made by every generation for those who would follow thereafter. "The valleys have been filled in, the mountains and hills have been made low, the crooked roads have been straightened, and the rough ways have been made smooth."

My maternal grandfather, a builder by trade, died several years before I was born. However, long before his demise his good deeds had become legendary in the small Florida hamlet where he lived. Like most people of his generation he was marked by the dark economic times simply referred to as "The Great Depression". During those lean years men and women did whatever they had to do out of sheer instinct to survive. Some turned to crime; others to alcohol. My Grandfather Rogers turned to God.

One of the folksy parables that he often recounted was about a man who owned a construction company. Because of the Great Depression the construction industry was at an all-time low and the young builder was almost bankrupt. His construction company was soon to be sold.

However, he had just married into a rather wealthy family that had somehow dodged the financial losses plaguing the general populace. Although his new father-in-law would probably have loaned or even given him money, the newly married builder was too proud to admit his need. So he continued to put on a charade, even though financial disaster was getting closer by the day.

Then all of a sudden the father-in-law decided that he wanted to build a new house for himself and his wife. He asked his new son-in-law to be the contractor. He instructed him, "Look, son, I want you to spare no expense on our house. Build it strong and build it well. Build it like you were building it for yourself and your wife, my daughter. Build it to last. I trust you. Just give me the bill when it is finished."

So the builder came up with a master plan for the new home. As he started to figure out the cost for the project it occurred to him that his in-laws were elderly and might not live too much longer. In fact, he reasoned, if he skimped here and there – if he used products that wouldn't last a long time, but would last just long enough to match the projected lifespans of his in-laws, he could garner an even greater profit margin. It wouldn't hurt anyone, he told himself. His in-laws would be dead and gone before the results of using inferior products became evident. The next owners would buy a poorly made house, but who cared about them? So, he set out to build a so-so house, one that would look good for the number of years he calculated his in-laws would live, though not much longer.

When the house was finished it looked great from the outside. It would be a long time before the façade gave way. The father-in-law was delighted with the outcome. He was even more delighted because he had commissioned the house to be built for his son-in-law and daughter as a late wedding gift. As he handed the key to his speechless son-in-law the older man said: "Mom and I wanted to give you two something for your wedding that would outlive us. We knew that you have a reputation for building houses that are sturdy and strong. So we didn't let you in on our little secret. You see, the house you built wasn't actually for us; it was for you and our daughter. Congratulations. We hope you enjoy your new house."

This story speaks to every generation. We aren't just walking the Extra Mile road; we are building and repairing it as we go for those who will follow in our footsteps. The father-in-law did the right thing by his generation, but his son-in-law did not. The father-in-law was an Extra Mile man who thought he was leaving behind an Extra Mile highway – one with no bumps, potholes, or discernable defects. His goal was thwarted because the younger man passed on inferior construction; an outwardly beautiful but inwardly crumbling edifice. In so doing his efforts were merely a mirage, and ill-advised foolishness.

This is today's challenge to all current Extra Mile pilgrims: Fill in the holes and straighten the road. Let's not just walk our own Extra Mile. Let's fix the path for those who will follow as we walk ever onward.

Hikers have a motto: "Leave nothing behind but footprints." To that let's add a codicil: "...and a straight, improved road on which the next generation can leave their footprints, too."

Chapter 30: Extra-Milers Rarely Go a Third Mile

Carry each other's burdens...
... each one should carry his [or her] own load.
~ Galatians 6:2, 5

Secret #30

If one mile is good, an Extra Mile is better, right?

Absolutely! Jesus introduced us to the Extra Mile concept – and it works. The philosophy is to go over and beyond the requirement of duty. The theology is to follow in the footsteps of Jesus, who shows us the way by his life and example. It is never acceptable to merely do the minimum. We should go all out, be all in, at every level of endeavor, great or small, all of the time.

This raises an important question: If two miles are so much better than one mile, why not go three miles? Why stop at two? Indeed, why should we stop at all – short of exhaustion, blisters, or breaking a leg on the extended journey? Even as there are ultra-marathoners, shouldn't there be ultra-Extra-Milers?

Let's drop the centurion's knapsack we are carrying for a moment and consider these questions. Let's lean back in the shade of a big rock, take a swig from our canteens, and mull the matter over. The math is rather simple: one mile is a requirement – the Extra Mile is the reward. The first mile is about the head; the Extra Mile is about the heart. The single mile may keep us from getting fired; the Extra Mile may get us promoted. It is intriguing that Jesus mandated only one extra mile – not two or three or a dozen additional miles. So, why do we stop at the Extra Mile marker? Why not go on and on and on?

When my younger brother was five years old he loved pumpkin pie. His idea of heaven was a place where he could eat pumpkin pie around-the-clock. So, one year before Thanksgiving Day dinner he snuck into the kitchen and consumed, not merely a large slice of his favorite pie, but a whole pie. Needless to say, a few minutes later he was quite ill. As a result, he cannot stand the sight or smell of pumpkin pie to this very day. One slice would have been good, two slices might have been better, but more proved to be far too much. He exceeded the tipping point and went from hungry to full to stuffed. He should have stopped at full.

The Apostle Paul writes that we should carry our brother's and our sister's burdens. However, a couple of verses later he seems to contradict himself when he advocates that every person should shoulder his or her own load. Is Paul confused or conflicted? Which is it: Should we carry or not carry a fellow pilgrim's pack for a third mile? Do we or don't we surprise the centurion who summons on a whim by going the unrequired and unexpected additional mile?

Actually, Paul's instructions are neither contradictory nor confused. Let's say that a man has an injured leg. He can barely walk much less lug a knapsack. So, it is only reasonable for us to help him for a while. During the season of recovery we walk the Extra Mile with him – slowly. We cater to both his diminished speed and lessened stamina. Sometimes we pamper the sojourner with the handicap. We get him ice cream or do his errands. In the meantime, the injured person grows stronger. Finally, he is completely well. He is given a bill of good health; he can get back to work again. The strained leg has mended and he is ready to shoulder his own load once more.

So, we stop at the Extra Mile marker to try and return the knapsack to the fellow, and we plan to go back to the trailhead and help someone else who is hurt and in need of assistance. But the now-healthy man doesn't want to carry his own pack. He has become accustomed to being served. He likes being pampered. Even though he no longer walks with a literal crutch, he prefers a companion to be his psychological, emotional, or financial crutch. He has joined the host of one-milers who spell service "serve us".

To go a third mile with such a person is to enable, not help. After the Extra Mile the average centurion, pilgrim, or friend should pick up his or her own pack. Indeed, after the Extra Mile the contagious spirit of ministry should cause the one who was once served to want to serve others, to return the favor and pass the blessing on to someone else. Going a third mile destroys the initiative that motivates us to serve others instead of always demanding to be the one served.

My mother was an avid Extra-Miler. She was the first to reach in her purse to help a needy person, to bring a covered dish to a sick neighbor, or to give a ride to a friend. However, she also set wise boundaries. She had her limits. It wasn't because she ever tired of serving. It was because she knew the trap of serving people who have come to the place where they can take care of themselves, but don't want to do so. After walking the Extra Mile with a needy person, she knew the wisdom of expecting him or her to start taking up the slack and the sack again. She went over and beyond when it was called for, but she also believed in shared responsibility. My mother, helper that she was, seldom went the third mile.

She taught me this by way of little things – such as insisting that I make my own bed, clean my own room, and do chores. Whereas some mothers did virtually everything for their children, my mother transferred her Extra Mile behavior to me by saying "let me do this for you", followed by "now let's do this together", and ultimately "now you can go help someone else". In retrospect, she did me a great favor. Some of my young friends and classmates grew up with a sense of entitlement because the key people in their lives believed in going the third mile for them. In so doing they created dependency instead of self-reliance. So, the third mile should be the exception rather than the rule.

Several years ago a young medical student attended our church. He and I were about the same size. So, when my clothes had become gently used I offered them to him. Sometimes I would throw in a new shirt or fresh tie in as well. I dressed him from the time he was a pre-med student until he became a successful surgeon.

After he had been in practice for a while he came to me one day and said, "You gave me many of your clothes when I was a student. You essentially dressed me. Now that I'm doing well financially I'd like to take you out and buy you some new clothes. Where would you like to go and what would you like me to get for you? Just name it and it's yours."

What was my response? Well, I certainly didn't turn him down! I didn't say, "No, no, no, it is my assignment to dress you for life." I was proud of the fact that he had learned how to be an Extra-Miler. He had come to the place where he was prepared to help others, even as he had been helped. It would have been unhealthy for me to be a third miler and insist on giving him more of my clothes when he had the wherewithal to dress both himself and me. He needed to learn how to share his resources, his gifts, and his time. I had helped him by going the Extra Mile with him - now it was his turn to help someone else.

At that moment I wasn't in need of any new clothes, however I did have a ministerial intern who didn't have a suit to his name. So, I pointed him out across the sanctuary and said, "Doc, if you want to serve me, serve him. Take that young man out this week and buy him the clothes you would have bought for me. Treat him as well as you intended to treat me. Go the Extra Mile with him instead of me." And that's what he did. In so doing, all three of us benefited – the doctor, the intern and me. We kept true to Extra Mile behavior without becoming enablers.

Consider this: In a relay race four people do in succession what one person usually does alone. Instead of a single athlete running 400 meters, four athletes run 100 meters apiece. They share the responsibility and they excel. They all do something to the best of their ability but no one does everything; the responsibility is shared.

When a person seeks to obtain a mortgage loan, the bank almost always expects the prospective homeowner to bring a percentage of the total to the closing. Why is this? Any respectable bank can certainly afford to front the total amount. The rationale is simple: Banks have found that shared responsibility between the lender and the borrower eventuates in much better chances of the loan being repaid. When the borrower has "skin in the game" at the outset there is a healthy attitude of mutual ownership and duty between the parties. Borrowers are less likely to default on a loan in which they have invested their own resources.

The fine line between going the second and the third mile isn't about distance as much as attitude. You can't measure where one starts and ends. It is more an art than a science.

Should a parent pay for a child's full college education – or should she pay some of it? Is it wise to always pick up the tab when going out to eat with friends – even when we can afford it? Must we be at the beck and call of demanding clients 24/7 – or are there times when our family needs us more than the company does? Does being an Extra-Miler require us to sacrifice our marriage, health, resources, retirement, and personal goals in the pursuit of superior service?

The place where we most often go awry is not as we traverse the Extra Mile, but when we venture into the realm of the third mile. It is there that we are run ragged, lose our joy, become depressed, and too frequently also lose our way. It is there that boundaries become blurred and we may feel prevailed upon.

An executive who recently lost his job remarked to me, "I gave my life to the company for 30 years and was then unexpectedly and unceremoniously escorted off the property because of a downsizing move." He admitted that he had been going the third mile for his company – where compulsive workaholism is taken for granted and disappointments looms just over the horizon.

Indeed, in general it is just as unproductive to walk the third mile as to settle for the single mile. Neither leads to the desired results. One is too little; the other is too much. The first mile is where we rust out, whereas the third mile is where we burn out. The Extra Mile is the ideal, the golden mean, the preferred goal.

In the days when ships were made of wood there was a rule of thumb: If a nearby ship was on fire then it was reasonable to offer to help put out the fire. However, there were limits. The captain of the safe vessel was not to venture too close. He was not to go to the point where his own ship was set ablaze from the heat.

Likewise, the best goal is the Extra Mile – not the first or the third. It is unwise to become a casualty of either indolence or excess. We should strive for excellence, which is achieved as we travel Mile 2. Let's valiantly recommit to walk two miles with our clients, customers, colleagues, family, neighbors, and friends. Let's make it our norm to consistently exceed first mile behavior. However, when we get to the end of the Extra Mile let's give the knapsack back to the original owner. It is then time for us to help another centurion. Why? Because each of us should ultimately be taught to carry his or her own load.

In summation, we should help to bear one another's burdens – that is, until the person who's been temporarily disabled can bear his or her own burden again. We should help people who are in financial need, but not perpetually. We should lend a listening ear to a brokenhearted friend, but not to where their bitterness and negativity infects us, too. Extra-Milers should do a lot, but not try to do everything. The Roman centurion shouldn't get too comfortable and we shouldn't become doormats in the process.

So, let's walk the Extra Mile – Mile 2 – and then go back to the trailhead to help other pilgrims, rather than merely enable the ones who can now bear their own load, and struggle with a burden that is now rightfully theirs.

One mile isn't enough; two miles is about right; three miles creates dependents.

Pilgrims, let's stick with the middle distance – the Extra Mile.

Chapter 31: Extra-Milers Meet at Trail's End

His master replied, 'Well done, good and faithful
servant! You have been faithful with a few things; I
will put you in charge of many things. Come and
share your master's happiness!'
~ Matthew 25:23

Secret #31

Money makes a good reward, but is a poor motivator.

You can give a lazy employee a raise, but don't expect better job performance as a direct result. You will be disappointed. Admittedly it may improve in the short term, but not over the long haul. You cannot pay a do-the-minimum one-miler to consistently and joyfully hike the Extra Mile, not for any price. Money changes lax behavior marginally and temporally at best. A tip won't improve a bad waiter, but it may make a good waiter better. Transformed attitudes can't be bought or bribed, only rewarded.

On the other hand, an already superior worker will strive for excellence if she is acknowledged or he is applauded by way of a bonus. A person with a deeply rooted sense of responsibility will improve because of appreciation. Encouragement makes most people want to hike further and go higher.

Of course, not everyone desires the same form of recognition. There are some people who aren't moved much by money, but they will go to great lengths for prizes, trophies, kind words, extra days off, a trip, a larger office, or some other form of recompense. An Extra-Miler doesn't mainly work for gain, but some sort of honor goes a long way to put a smile on his or her face. Therefore, those who lead Extra Mile people should strive to find out what motivates each person who is on their Extra Mile team.

Jesus told a story about a man who was going on a trip. He called three trusted servants and gave each of them a bag of gold coins. To the first servant he gave five coins, to the second he gave two, and to the last man he gave one. His departing instructions were clear: "Increase my investment." He didn't tell them how to do the job; he simply told them to get it done. The workers were required to figure out the details for themselves. He expected creative initiative on their part, not mere obedience or acquiescence to a set of narrow preset instructions.

The first man went to work and doubled the money almost immediately, as did the second fellow. However, the third man, the one who had received a single gold coin, dug a hole in the ground and hid it. He didn't invest it, put in the bank, or try to make a windfall in the stock market with it. He was lazy. He lacked spunk and was unacceptably conservative in his approach to life. He was a first miler. His unwillingness to take a chance with his single gold coin was actually symptomatic of his bored, uneventful, and risk adverse existence. He was content with the status quo. His rationale was that his master wouldn't chide him if he didn't lose the coin. Though he wouldn't be rewarded, neither would he be punished. He lived by the adage: "Better safe than sorry." As it turned out, he was wrong.

Single-milers are like the one-coin man in Jesus' parable. They may go through life without getting into trouble, but neither do they succeed greatly. They take no risks but they make no gains. They live in the vast wasteland of gray hues and subdued colors. Yes, they walk the enforced single mile with the centurion but they grumble all the way and thereby miss the beautiful terrain in the process. Then they loop back and do it again. Their vista and perspective never changes because their attitude remains the same and they do what they've always done, thus they get what they always got before.

So, in Jesus' story the master came home, called his three workers together, and asked them to account for what they had done with his gold coins. The first two proudly announced that they had doubled their investment. They laid before the boss their increase – the five coins that had become ten and the two coins that had become four.

Wonderful! Now how about the man who had been given one coin to invest? He emerged rather sheepishly from the shadows, cautiously opened up his silk handkerchief, and laid before his boss the single coin he'd been given months before. He waited for his employer's response. He knew he would not be commended, but he didn't think he would be condemned. After all, he had not lost the coin. The company was no worse off than before. He wouldn't be promoted, but neither would he be put down.

Alas, he was in for a big surprise. The CEO pursed his lips and was silent for a few moments. Then he became angry. He didn't yell and scream, but it was clear that he was very unhappy. From between clenched teeth he said: "Why didn't you at least put the money in the bank? Perhaps you wouldn't have doubled the investment, but at least you would have something to show me for your effort. You have done nothing, so you will get nothing. So now give your coin to the man over there that has ten coins. He's an Extra-Miler and you're not. Oh, and by the way, you're fired!"

Shortly thereafter the leader gave an awards banquet for the two top workers, the ones who had doubled his investment. In his speech he commended them, promoted them, and made them fully vested members of his firm. He told them that from now on whenever he made a profit, they would make a profit. They would share in his happiness. They were now platinum card-carrying members of the Extra Mile Club.

All the while the unemployed one-coin fellow was sitting at home, licking his wounds, nursing a grudge, and muttering that no one ever gave him a break.

One-milers are like that. Most often they fail to see the correlation between their minimal effort and the corresponding unremarkable results. However, when they do make the connection a whole new panorama opens up before them. Instead of stopping at exactly the one-mile marker they forge ahead on the Extra Mile path. Life begins to change for the better, not merely in the arena of employment but in every area, every day and in every way.

We have been traversing the Extra Mile together for quite a while now. Along the way we've discovered some secrets that have emerged naturally while hiking the Extra Mile trail. We've moved from doing what we must on the first mile to accomplishing what we want to on the Extra Mile.

St. Augustine is credited with the saying: "Love God and do as you will." Once we've settled on the right attitude the correct actions will follow naturally. If we are genuine from-the-heart Extra-Milers we'll do the right thing for those we serve – or at least try valiantly to do so. If here and there, now and then, we get off the pathway we'll soon get back on it again.

I imagine that one-milers of old used to gather at the end of the first mile to discuss the injustice of Roman laws, to talk in bitter tones about the centurion who had disrupted their day by compelling them to carry his knapsack. They would lean against the milestone and say: "Here and not an inch further!" Then they would return to the place where they had started from, the point of origin, and do it all over again. Their only means of controlling life was by way of establishing what they wouldn't do, rather than what they could and would do.

On the other hand, in my mind's eye I can see and hear the Extra-Milers meeting around the two-mile marker to chat as well. However, as I listen in on their conversation their words are animated, excited, and positive. They aren't talking about what they were forced to do along the way, but what they wanted to do.

I hear one pilgrim say: "I admit it – I was unfulfilled throughout the first mile. But then something happened – the idea of the Extra Mile kicked in. Now I don't have problems with Roman soldiers. In fact, I am thankful for them. They have taught me a valuable lesson about how to go over and beyond."

Another breaks in: "You're right, friend. I don't know how often I walked merely one begrudging mile with an arrogant centurion before I learned the power of the Extra Mile. When I quit insisting on my rights and started serving others willingly my life changed for the better. I'm glad I'm not part of the One Mile Worker's Union any longer. I'm grateful for my Extra Mile Club gold card!"

Every day there are meetings across the world at both the one-mile and the two-mile markers. The items on the agendas for both meetings look the same – marriage, family, work, education, community service, church, government, and so on. However, the approach at the two meetings is completely different. One is about complaining; the other is about gaining. The first mile is about doing the minimum; the Extra Mile is about going for the maximum. When the meetings end, the pursuant actions and results are quite different. One-milers try to avoid the centurion, whereas Extra-Milers seek to engage him. One shirks; the other works.

Two brothers were going off to summer camp for a week. Before they left they asked their mother for some money to buy candy, soft drinks, and incidentals while away. She replied that she would give them the requested money, on the condition that they promised her to read a chapter from a book she was putting in their luggage every day that they were at camp. The brothers didn't like to read, but they rather reluctantly complied. She then packed a book into each of their suitcases.

On the bus going to the camp one brother realized that his mother had not given him any money. She had apparently forgotten her promise and not kept her word. So, throughout that week he did not open the book she had given him, much less read from it. If she hadn't done her part, why should he do his? He was quite upset because while his fellow campers were plying themselves with sweets and sodas, he was going without. He would have words with his mother when he returned home. His week had been ruined by her neglect and forgetfulness.

The other brother made a similar discovery when he arrived at camp. His mother had apparently forgotten to give him the promised allowance, too. However, he took a different approach. He decided to do his part even though his mother had not seemingly kept her agreement. When he opened the book she had packed for him he discovered that there, as a bookmark, was a crisp $50 bill. His mother had not forgotten after all! Needless to say, his week had a considerably different outcome than his brother's.

When we do our part, no matter what anyone else may do, we are Extra-Milers. When we go over and beyond, even though others around us are not, we are on the Extra Mile journey. When we are no longer hiking because the centurion has forced us to do so, when we are walking out of desire rather than compulsion, we have started to learn the secrets of Mile 2 living. If we will keep our part of the promise we may find that everything else will work out, too.

An old adage says: "Birds of a feather flock together." Two kinds of hikers and pilgrims on the road of life also tend to congregate around their respective mile markers.

In New England, where I live, when you go from rural to urban areas there are signs that warn "Thickly Settled". The first mile is, indeed, thickly populated. There are so many people on it at times that movement is slow and tedious. However, when you go beyond the requirement of the first mile the traffic lanes begin to narrow. There is less congestion on the Extra Mile. The hikers are fewer and fewer the farther one goes on the winding blue ribbon of this unique, narrow roadway.

Finally, we can see the post that marks the end of the trail up ahead. While trekking the Extra Mile both you and the centurion you've been serving have been transformed. You will never be the same again and neither will the centurion. Amazingly, you actually thank the astounded soldier whose pack you've carried for being the instrument to teach you a series of valuable life lessons.

Now as we end our journey together, I want to say thanks for making this jaunt with a growing number of Extra-Milers and me. We've now come to the end of the trail, my friends. While there are more lessons to learn and more secrets to discover, this is it for now. So let's rest up and then start walking again soon – for two miles, always two miles.

* * *

MILE 2

Acknowledgements

Many Extra-Milers have contributed to this book, on purpose or otherwise. Indeed, I hesitate to start thanking this tribe of Mile 2 people out of a sense that I will certainly miss someone along the way. So, I'll keep it simple.

I am in debt to my parents who raised me, to the grandparents who loved me, to the teachers who taught me, to the pastors who shepherded me, and to the friends who have cared for me. Thank you all.

The congregations I have been honored to serve, the staff members who have served with me, and the small group that helped me sharpen the focus of this book all have gone over and beyond the call of duty.

I want to thank Shari Risoff, my ultra-encouraging and ever-cheerful Extra Mile editor; Thomas Snelling, the photographer who took the photo on the back of the book jacket and did so much with so little; and Brian Godawa, the creative book cover designer.

My wife and our immediate and extended family have all turned out to be Extra-Milers of the first order. I am so proud of them. They challenge me to do better every day.

And I want to thank you, the reader of this book. One-half of all profits will go toward helping needy people get closer to the Extra Mile. They thank you for making this possible.

Finally, I thank God that He went the Extra Mile for me, for all of us. Where would we be without the Via Dolorosa? That winding road is still the ultimate Mile 2.

About the Author

Rogers Steven (Steve) Warner serves as the Lead Pastor of the Brockton Assembly of God in Brockton, Massachusetts. The church is noted for its cultural diversity, with more than 30 nationalities represented within the congregation.

Steve has ministered in over 25 countries and has been the senior pastor of four churches: Maranatha Chapel in Evergreen Park, IL: planted 1975 and pastored for 23 years; Oakbrook Community Church, Oakbrook, IL; Interim Lead Pastor of The Stone Church, Palos Heights, IL. He also served for 28 years as a board member of Illinois Teen Challenge and on numerous other boards throughout the years.

He holds an MA degree in Communications from Wheaton College, Wheaton, IL and a Doctor of Ministry degree from Trinity International University in Deerfield, IL. He previously held the position of Vice President of Marketing with Christian Communications of Chicagoland, which purchased and operated Channel 38 in Chicago (known today as Total Living Network).

Steve has been both married and a credentialed minister for over 46 years. He and his wife, Vickie have four children (Tamara, Sean, Tiffany, and Courtney), and six grandchildren (Theo, Warner, Maddie, Annie, Fletcher, and Riley).

His avocations include collecting books, fountain pens, signatures, and rare documents. Steve enjoys road trips in his convertible, biking, kayaking, and hiking. In the process of his travels he has visited all 50 states and almost as many countries, enjoying numerous adventures along the way.

His main life goal continues to be to glorify the Lord Jesus by both knowing Him personally and making Him known to others.

Steve Warner

MILE 2

Made in the USA
Lexington, KY
23 February 2016